life after breath

Life After Breath is an incredibly insightful book that speaks deeply to the heart and mind of the reader because it comes from the heart and life experience of the author. You will be drawn into Susan's personal story and the comforting sufficiency of God's Word.

Becoming a widow is never a personal choice. *Life After Breath* will give you strength, hope, and comfort. Its profound truth will draw you back again and again as you discover the purpose for which God has set you apart.

Perhaps you have questioned the meaning of your painful journey. This engaging book helps to clarify that journey with the light of God's Word.

Dr. H. Norman Wright, LMFT,Grief expert and award-winning author of more than seventy books
Tess Wright, Author of *The One-Minute Counselor for Women*

Poignant, transparent, lyrical, and gut-wrenchingly honest, *Life After Breath* is a gift to those who have experienced the deep sorrow of losing a loved one. Susan VandePol offers deep spiritual wisdom spoken with beauty and grace. I highly recommend this book to those who have experienced grief, as well as therapists, pastors, friends, and anyone who has ever wondered if it was possible to move beyond their suffering.

Shelly Beach, Award-winning author, speaker, caregiving expert, and co-founder of PTSDPerspectives.com

What an amazing story of courage and healing! Susan VandePol has clearly articulated the tender moments of her grief journey, painting beautiful word pictures and using memorable analogies to describe the horrific pain and helplessness of watching her beloved husband's struggle with Lou Gehrig's disease. In these pages you will find the hope, comfort, and healing found only in our Lord Jesus Christ.

Joseph Northcut, Director of Church Ministries,
GriefShare.org

Most people walking the planet today have experienced grief at some time in their lives, but most don't have the gift of words to put pen to paper the way that Susan VandePol does. *Life After Breath* is one of the most beautifully written expressions of grief I have ever read.

At once heartbreakingly honest and hope-filled, this book will be one of the first in my literary arsenal when I recommend a book about grief and healing.

Wanda Sanchez, PTSD consultant and publicist,
Co-author of *Love Letters from the Edge: Meditations for Those Struggling with Brokenness, Trauma, and the Pain of Life*

life
after breath

After Her Husband
Takes His Last Breath,
and After She Tries
to Catch Hers

Susan VandePol

TO Lois

Susan VandePol

 I s. 45:3

New York

life after breath
After Her Husband Takes His Last Breath, and After She Tries to Catch Hers

Published in New York, New York, by Morgan James Publishing. Morgan James and The Entrepreneurial Publisher are trademarks of Morgan James, LLC. www.MorganJamesPublishing.com

The Morgan James Speakers Group can bring authors to your live event. For more information or to book an event visit The Morgan James Speakers Group at www.TheMorganJamesSpeakersGroup.com.

ISBN 978-1-63047-342-6 paperback
ISBN 978-1-63047-343-3 eBook
ISBN 978-1-63047-344-0 hardcover
Library of Congress Control Number: 2014944166

A **free** eBook edition is available with the purchase of this print book.

CLEARLY PRINT YOUR NAME ABOVE IN UPPER CASE

Instructions to claim your free eBook edition:
1. Download the BitLit app for Android or iOS
2. Write your name in **UPPER CASE** on the line
3. Use the BitLit app to submit a photo
4. Download your eBook to any device

Cover Design by:
Rachel Lopez
www.r2cdesign.com

Interior Design by:
Bonnie Bushman
bonnie@caboodlegraphics.com

Back cover photo:
Wendy Swenson Photography

Cover art:
Ben Ortega

In an effort to support local communities, raise awareness and funds, Morgan James Publishing donates a percentage of all book sales for the life of each book to Habitat for Humanity Peninsula and Greater Williamsburg.

Get involved today, visit
www.MorganJamesBuilds.com

Habitat for Humanity
Peninsula and
Greater Williamsburg
Building Partner

Robert Miranda Ortega
December 26, 1952–April 7, 2005

Contents

Prologue

I've always known the power of a story. Maybe I've always seen life word by word and page by page; I don't know for sure. There are those moments that define a life. They are your moments, but they are not meant for you alone. They help others. It is a mystery of sorts. When someone hears another's story—maybe your story or even mine—they can finally exhale and lean back into their own narrative. It always seems to involve breathing and depends on the circumstance to determine the depth of its expression. Sometimes the moment is communicated with a gasp or sigh or moan of agony or pain. It may be the exhale after a good laugh or cry. It may be the moment the doctor gives you the news. The moment the doctor gave me the news. The moment my husband took his last breath, and the kids and I tried to catch ours and say good-bye.

Others need to breathe, and they need our air, our story, so that they can breathe too.

One

Catching Your Breath

And Jesus uttered a loud cry, and breathed His last.
Mark 15:37 NASB

he pauses grew longer in between each heaving effort to live, and then he breathed his last. My husband died on a rainy afternoon in April . . . and we said good-bye.

I'm holding my breath now, years later as I write and remember, and as I wonder about what circumstances brought you here to this book, to this page. I can almost see you; it seems you are holding your breath too. We are both here for the same reason. Your husband has taken his last breath, and you loved him. Me too.

After God formed Adam from the dust of the ground, He "breathed into his nostrils the breath of life; and man became a living being" (Genesis 2:7 NASB). Jesus Himself knows what it is to take a first breath, and He knows what it is to take His last. We get our word *breath* from the Latin word *spiritus*, meaning "life" or "spirit." In Hebrew, the word *ruach* means "breath" and is also translated into English as "spirit." In the New Testament, the Greek *pneuma* is most often translated as the "Holy Spirit," but it is also used to describe breathing in and out through one's nostrils or mouth. In this way, breath is the vital principle that animates a body; it is both the first sign of life and the last. A person's spirit, his breath, moves in and out and through his essence and represents the human power of knowing, desiring, deciding, and acting.[1] *Pneuma* is also used to "describe a soul that has left the body."[2]

The Spirit is like the wind, the Bible says—we cannot see it or know where it comes from and where it is going, but we can see and feel its effects. Your husband's life, the breath of his spirit, lingers, conjuring up the same feeling, even though he is not here anymore. You feel his presence profoundly. The throbbing fever of it seems inescapable, but hold fast Believer; the omnipresent Spirit of your Savior reigns in the transactions of life, breath, death, and circumstance. Your Christ is breathing for you.

The Spirit led Jesus into the wilderness, where you are now.

"But He is God," you say.

Yes, and He's breathing for you.

You are broken, but so was He.

He breathes for you.

Your heart died with your husband.

Jesus died too, but He conquered death and rose again.

He's breathing for you, Believer.

He cried out with a loud voice in the last moments before He breathed his last.

You want to scream and cry out too. Do it. He's breathing for you.

Dear Grieving Friend, to live, breathing is involved. His breath, His Spirit, His life will continue to course into yours. You will inhale and exhale again without catching your breath continuously on the jagged edge of your pain. You will catch your breath and live because your God is the God of the living and the dead, and whether we live or die, we do it for Him. He will do the breathing for you.

Job's friend, the faithful Elihu, reminded him, "The Spirit of God hath made me, and the breath of the Almighty hath given me life" (Job 33:4 NASB). The apostle Paul passionately reminds us, "In Him we live and move and exist" (Acts 17:28 NASB). Jesus told His disciples, "Apart from Me you can do nothing" (John 15:5 NASB), and to ensure their success, the Spirit, the breath, the *ruach* of truth, would be left with them forever as their "Comforter, Counselor, Helper, Intercessor, Advocate, Strengthener, and Standby" (John 14:16 AMP). They would know Him because He would always abide with them. He would be as close as their own breath because He *was* their breath. For you, My Friend, whether you whisper, gasp, or scream, He is there with you, in you, and for you.

God is immeasurably entrenched in your grief, and His compassion never ceases or fails to do what it set out to accomplish (Lamentations 3:22–23). The compassion of God means He is *co*-passionate with you. He feels with you and *co*-suffers with you— literally. It was His passion that brought Him to earth and led Him to the cross, and it is His passion that left His Spirit here to keep you breathing. It heals you, sustains you, restores you, and anoints you for the task at hand.

It will take some time . . . probably a long time; don't let anyone kid you or dismiss the agony or longevity of grief, because where the Spirit of the Lord is—the source of your breath—there is freedom, and that means freedom to grieve. The loss is worthy of the effort and honor.

So here we begin: your life after his last breath. There may have been a time when you rested your head on his chest and felt his breath on your cheek. Unless he was snoring or had eaten garlic, those moments were sacred and very, very personal. Maybe you remember when your child was so frail and small that to be certain they were breathing, you leaned your ear close to their sweet mouth and heard their breath and felt the whisper of it on your skin. The breath of the Almighty is ever so much more personal, more intimate. It is full of promise and seals His pledge of faithfulness to you. Lean in, rest your head on His chest, listen, and feel His breath on your wet cheek. See His thumbs wipe your tears as He holds your face in His hands. With every turn of these pages, the rustle of air between them will remind you of His presence. Breathe.

The Lord God created the heavens and stretched them out. He shaped the earth and all that comes from it. He gave life to the people who are on it and breath to those who walk on it. This is what the Lord God says: I, the Lord, have called you to do what is right. I will take hold of your hand. I will protect you.

Isaiah 42:6–7 GWT

Two

Crying in the Shower

*Crying is all right in its way while it lasts. But you have
to stop sooner or later, and then you still have to decide
what to do.*

—**C. S. Lewis**, *The Silver Chair*

he kids weren't home to stay with their dad, but it was still
early enough in his disease that I could run out and attend
to the regular duties of life while he took a shower. Bob had
just been diagnosed with Lou Gehrig's disease—a fatal condition
that leads to paralysis, where patients eventually cannot breathe
or swallow. (There's that "breathing" thing again.) Like the

6

ticks of a clock in a classroom, life for us was now measured by hands we could not control. The sound of their movement became louder and heavier as we watched, and to be honest, recess sounded pretty good already. The problem was, class had just started, and it was to be an extended education in a foreign language we would never master.

We had begun the necessity of grieving but were (as of yet) unfamiliar with its moods, though later we would learn intimately of its care, sanctuary, and friendship. Not today though. I had forgotten my grocery list, and after pulling back into the driveway, walking through the garage door, and into the house to find where I had left it, I heard something. It sounded like screaming and sobbing all at the same time—breathless sobbing. To hear it that day froze my soul and took my breath too. Bob was screaming, asking God "why, why, why?" begging for the cup to pass from him, and hitting his open-palmed hand as hard as he could against the tile wall of the shower. Death would take him eventually, and this was his first protest. It was a lament kicking against the permanent kidnapping of his life.

I ran to our bathroom, pulled back the shower curtain, and turned the water off. Grabbing a towel, I wrapped him up, dried him off, held him tight, and cried. It was the first time of many that I would steady him like that over those next three years. We all did a lot of that—still do for each other. I realized that I had no idea what to do, but as C. S. Lewis said, I still had to decide. So I got Bob dressed, waited until he was calm, and . . . went to the market for groceries. Odd. I felt like I had failed, and it wouldn't be the last time. I'll be honest. Something inside me wanted to run. Not exactly the loving thing to do. I didn't run, though. Love doesn't. It stays behind with the beloved.

We were all held hostage by sin's verdict, but Jesus submitted to the Father, drank the cup, and gave the Holy Spirit to stay with us. Love stays. It just does.

Dear Grieving Believer, you have cried and pounded your fist of emotions on the hard surface of death in protest too. The cup did not pass you by, but here in what feels like a deserted place is where you will discover that Love has not left you. The cup did not pass Him by either, but He didn't run then and He will not run from you now in your greatest hour of need. He is here, though the night is dark and you do not know what to do. He made the first decision for you: to stay. Love stays; it just does.

There was a night in a garden, Lord, when You begged too, and I wonder if it involved pounding Your hand on something in holy protest. Sin would not hold You because it could not separate Love from its beloved with the sting of death. We are separated from Bob now, but because of You, the separation is not permanent. Thank You for such a victory. Thank You that I will never have to hear his scream again. I'm grateful that I didn't have to hear Your scream that day when You were in agony beyond description and crying out to the Father. Neither You nor Bob will ever have to suffer like that again, and the next time I hear Your shout, it will be on that great day of reconciliation and reunion, when there will be no more suffering, no more pain, and no more crying in the shower.

"Because of the devastation of the afflicted, because of the groaning of the needy, now I will arise," says the Lord; "I will set him in the safety for which he longs."

Psalm 12:5 NASB

Three

Bury Your Face

Sometimes, and for different reasons, we cover our faces with our hands. Different parts of our faces: our mouths, our eyes, or the whole thing. If something surprises us, our first reaction is to put our hands over our mouth. It can be a way to momentarily hide or escape a painful inevitability. In church on occasion, I cover my face with my hands during worship or prayer. It helps me to focus and keep away distraction. Sometimes we raise our hands in disbelief or set our hands on top of our heads or in our hair with emotion. I've seen a lot of men in particular do that, especially over a bad call during a sporting event, accompanied with "You've got to be kidding me!"

This gesture seems to involve situations where we know we have no control. It seems to happen when the word *no* is racing through our mind. It definitely happens after holding our breath and then letting out a response that is raw, originating in our soul and surfacing after hearing news of the unthinkable. It's accompanied by numbness or a sickening sensation that our soul has been scraped by a metal spatula over a cast-iron skillet.

The morning after the neurologist gave us the diagnosis, I slipped out of bed without any sleep under my belt and walked into the living room. I stood there not knowing what to do, feeling numb and scraped clean. Bob was still asleep, so I went to do what required no thinking: the laundry. I walked into the small room and was drawn immediately to the line of jackets and sweatshirts hanging on hooks to my right. They were Bob's, for the most part. He wore them when he was outside working in the yard or in the garage doing guy things. He wore them to play outside with the kids. These were the ones that had the dirt and aroma of life all over them. In my memory, they are vivid with worn color even now: plaid, flannel, Dodger blue, gray and stained, and a down jacket with a hole covered by duct tape to keep the feathers from escaping.

I fell apart and buried my face. Not in my hands this time, but in the jackets and sweatshirts. I wrapped my arms around them all, pressed my grief into their embrace, and cried. As I breathed in to catch my breath, I could smell him. I could smell my husband. Everybody has a scent, so to speak. It was like perfume to me, and I buried my face and heaving emotions even deeper into their hold. It wasn't a pretty thing; it was desperate, unladylike crying. I didn't have a lace hanky to wipe my face, just his sleeves, and I didn't want to pull away from the comfort I found in the scent of my husband. The Lord surprised me there in an unexpected place. He continuously does that in His kindness and grace when we are broken and stripped of our own efforts.

I went back to our room and slid in next to him. Wrapping my arms around his deteriorating body, I put my face into the crook of his neck and breathed him in.

Breath of heaven, hold me together, be forever near me, breath of heaven.

Chris Eaton

Four

The Aroma of Grief

But thanks be to God who always leads us in triumph in Christ, and manifests through us the sweet aroma of the knowledge of Him in every place. For we are a fragrance of Christ to God among those who are being saved and among those who are perishing; to the one an aroma from death to death, to the other an aroma from life to life. And who is adequate for these things?

2 Corinthians 2:14–16 NASB

The day began to unfold and unravel, and grief in its infancy was still holding its breath. The aroma of the early morning wafted through my senses, and I headed to the shower. As I stepped in I heard something. It wasn't screaming this time. It was the Lord, and His voice was soft and as clear as I have ever heard it. He said,

"Susan, I love you so much. Your prayers are such a fragrant aroma to Me, I could bury My face in them. Pray."

The tender intensity of His words is difficult to describe. Suffice it to say that early on in my conversion I learned that prayer is an apprehended and consumed heart, ever before the Father, whose expression and conversation is never to cease once it has begun. The apostle Paul asked the proverbial question, "And who is adequate for these things?"

Certainly not me. So I prayed. From then on I prayed with the tangible knowledge that the living God buried His Son and raised Him victorious so that He could bury His face in my prayers—and in yours too, Dear Hurting Friend. *Pray.*

Not that we are adequate in ourselves to consider anything
as coming from ourselves, but our adequacy is from God.
2 Corinthians 3:5 NASB

Five

More Smells

We were at McDonald's recently and ended up discussing why they seem to have a corner on the best-tasting fries, so we Googled it. (God is everywhere; even McDonald's.) We found out that the world's largest flavor companies also manufacture the scents of most of the best-selling perfumes, not to mention the scents of most household products like shampoo, furniture polish, and deodorant. Scientists say the human sense of smell is not fully understood and is greatly influenced by psychological factors and expectations. They also say that aroma and memory are inextricably linked, a fact God ordained for His purpose and fast-food chains use to their advantage.

Our taste buds offer us little help in identifying exactly what it is we are tasting as compared to our olfactory senses, which can perceive thousands of different aromas. Flavor is largely determined by the smell of gases released by the simple act of chewing. The gases follow a passageway in the back of your mouth to a layer of nerve cells called the olfactory epithelium, located at the base of your nose right between your eyes. Your brain combines the complexities from your olfactory epithelium with the simple taste signals from your tongue, assigns a flavor to what's in your mouth, and gives you the verdict.

Somehow . . . *somehow* . . . while we bury our faces in grief and breathe in, and God, with love inexorable, buries His face in our prayers and breathes us in, we know that as our sacrifice burns on the altar of pain, it is received as a priceless gift of worship to Him—a rising aroma pleasing to our God. The fragrant aroma of you, so delightful to Him, can be translated as a soothing aroma. Believer, imagine. To soothe means to "ease or relieve." *Webster's* says that an aroma is a quality that can be perceived by the olfactory senses. It is a pleasant characteristic or a distinctive, intangible quality—an aura. You are, in your darkest hour, "the sweet fragrance of Christ exhaled unto God" (2 Corinthians 2:15 AMP), "the fragrant aroma of Christ" (NIV). You remind the Father of the inestimable sacrifice of His Son.

Beloved Saint, as you are doubled over and facedown in your sorrow, He sees you and He will remember. Your lament is a sweet savor of Christ to God. It is the offering, so to speak, that Jesus is continually making to God through you. He will remember. How could He forget?

> *God is not unjust so as to forget your work and love.*
> Hebrews 6:10 NASB

Six

On the Fourth Day

Y ou are splintered with the memories of the one who is gone. There is desperation, and grasping and clawing, and the bleeding won't stop. I don't know if you had time to say good-bye before your husband left you or not. Either way, something inside said no, didn't it? I think it's because we weren't meant to say good-bye. Death is supposed to rip our insides out. It is a result of holiness profaned. It won't fit in a file folder.

I said no. Even after God nestled His face into my soul, I said no. "I've given You everything! I will not say yes to this." I even said, "How could You?"

Different types of offerings are described in the Old Testament representing the communion between worshipper and God. Some sacrificial offerings were made as part of a social gathering or family meal, served as a way to show veneration and to give back to God what He had bestowed. A portion of the offering was given to God, and a portion was eaten by the family or community. But an *olah* offering was different in that no part of it was to be consumed by anyone but God. The term *olah* comes from a Hebrew word that means "to go up." An *olah* offering was completely burnt on the altar; nothing was left but ash, and even the ash was only His. It represented utter submission to God's will and was considered the highest level of communion between the one making the sacrifice and God.

The point is that the person who brought the *olah* offering was acting out of obedience and derived no personal benefit from it, unlike other offerings in which the person got to partake. The *olah* offering was an outward sign that the person was willing to be obedient to God even though they personally gained nothing from it. It was a purely sacrificial offering, no strings attached.

This is the "sweet aroma," the "fragrance" spoken of in 2 Corinthians 2:14–15. We are, in obedience, the sweet aroma of Him in every place and a fragrance of Christ to God. Oh my!

Theologian Albert Barnes described this kind of aromatic sacrifice as one that is made "manifest" through us and is "made known" and spread abroad just as a pleasant fragrance is diffused through the air.[3] The verb *diffuse* means to spread over a wide area or among a large number of people. The result is not concentrated or localized. It means to break up, distribute, and become transmitted, especially by contact. A surprising synonym for diffuse is *sow*, which literally means "to introduce into a new environment." When speaking of diffused light, we say that it is transmitted from a broad light source, or "reflected." Your grief has brought you into a new environment, and you will carry its reflection for the rest of your life because it is transmitted from *the* broad Light Source.

On the fourth day after my husband's diagnosis, I said yes to God. I couldn't tell you what happened between day one and day four except that during that time, we had to tell our three kids, family, friends, and coworkers that Bob had a disease for which there is no cure or treatment. My *olah* wasn't offered on the third day so that I could make a super spiritual resurrection connection, but then again, He is the only one worthy of all honor and praise and the only one to whom an *olah* is given on any day. He gives life on the third or the fourth day, and the only way to hack my way through the present pain and coming sorrow was to bow and say yes.

God is a consuming fire, so I stepped onto the altar, no strings attached. He consumed me and breathed in my offering. That offering continues to this day. In ancient times, the fire that burned on the altar after the *olah* offering was never allowed to go out because the ongoing sacrificial offerings provided constant material for its consumption; the same is true for ours.

Beloved, the consuming fire that is God serves many purposes. Today, for you, He is a warm flame of comfort and a conquering victor at the same time. He has conquered the enemies that would have consumed you first had He not stepped in. He consumes you this day to protect you. He consumes you to lead you in His triumphant procession over death and its pain so that you can share the victory of His sacrificial death and destruction of the grave. Draw near, Dear Believer. Draw near and know.

Know therefore today that it is the Lord Your God who is crossing over before you as a consuming fire.
Deuteronomy 9:3 NASB

Fear not: for I have redeemed thee, I have called thee by thy name; thou art mine.
Isaiah 43:1 KJV

Yea, I have loved thee with an everlasting love: therefore, with loving kindness have I drawn thee.
Jeremiah 31:3 KJV

When all the people saw it, they fell on their faces; and they said, "The Lord, He is God; the Lord, He is God."
1 Kings 18:39 NASB

Seven

The Procession

I n 2 Corinthians 2:14, Paul speaks of triumph before he mentions the aroma of our sacrifice. There is only one other place in the New Testament where this word *triumph* is used, and it refers to the triumph of Christ over sin and the enemy who brought it into the world. Colossians 2:14-15 (KJV) explains:

> . . . *blotting out the handwriting of ordinances that was against us, which was contrary to us, and took it out of the way, nailing it to the cross; and having spoiled*

principalities and powers, He made a show of them openly,
triumphing over them in it.

Both 2 Corinthians 2 and Colossians 2 describe the triumphal procession of a victorious general. The pomp and circumstance in a procession of such magnitude was unparalleled in Roman times and here ushers the believer's imagination to a scene of heavenly grandeur. On the occasion of the Roman triumph, all the temple doors were thrown open, garlands of flowers decorated every shrine and image, and incense smoked on every altar so that the victor was greeted with a cloud of perfume.

The successful general would enter the city draped in purple, drowned in gold and pearls, and mounted atop his chariot drawn by white horses, or on occasion a pair of elephants, lions, or tigers. His prisoners preceded him along the sacred way to the capital, where his captives would be sacrificed. Often his children and closest friends accompanied him, while behind him stood a slave holding a jeweled crown over his head. His infantry brought up the rear with their spears adorned in laurel. The spoils of war, including kings, princes, or generals taken in battle, were displayed and paraded while the citizens looked on, celebrating with shouts of triumph and singing.

What distinguishes God's triumph from that of a human general is that His captive is brought into *willing* obedience to Christ and so joins in the triumph. God leads him as one not merely "triumphed over," but as one also "triumphing over" his foes with God. In Luke 5:10, Jesus said to Peter, "Do not fear, from now on you will be catching men." Literally, that means to "take captive so as to preserve alive."

Dear Reader, the villain that keeps you on your knees and your heart broken and doubled over in the shadow of death is, in the irony of God, the very lawless, illegitimate, thieving criminal who you, along with your victorious King, will march in victory over on that great day. You will display your spoils of war. You will march in triumph. You will be forever reunited with love lost. The last enemy to be triumphed over is death, and the victory is yours. Beloved, you will join your Christ in banishing what seems so final now. The small racketeer who has defrauded you will bow and laugh no more. The one who stole from you will never steal again—never. You have hope; he does not. His blackmailing, hijacking, deceitful, deplorable, senseless ways will come to an end, and you will join God in ending it. There will be no more of his dirty, crooked, desperate corruption and no more pillaging of your life or anybody else's. Death is doomed—you are not.

Eight

Transition

transition:

Noun: the process or period of changing from one state or condition to another; a sudden, unprepared modulation. Change, often major.

Verb: to undergo or cause to undergo a process or period of transition.

Synonyms: passage, change, crossing, transit, alteration, growth, metamorphosis, progress, realignment, shift, transformation, turning point, upheaval.

I had been in labor for eighteen hours. This was my first child, and no one had come close to explaining what was going to happen to me. After the doctor decided my baby's vitals were showing signs that it may be time for a C-section, I was in *transition* for almost two hours. No class could have prepared me for this, just as no class could have prepared me for the transition of the deaths of my mom by suicide and my dad from cancer, my miscarried child, the tragic death of my childhood friend Robby, or that of my husband Bob.

Medically speaking, in labor, as the body begins to adjust to accommodate the last few centimeters of dilation, hormones rise to crazy levels and you know something has happened. Transition is the most intense part of birth, and it is the most intense part of death. In birth, as in death, exhaustion and emotions tell you to give up.

The physical signs of transition include shaking or trembling. The desire to eat is long gone at this point, and ice chips are the laborer's sustenance. All energy must be conserved for what is to come. Nausea or vomiting is common, as is sweating. Also accompanying transition is the inability to relax or be comfortable. Even if a woman was handling labor well to this point, now she has no idea what to do, and often neither does her husband. The classes they took and literature they read is of no use now. Here is when a woman is the most emotionally needy and feels out of control. Some need encouragement; some need their space; some need both. Some need more. Transition is not only for the mother's physical preparedness, but it is the preface to one of the two most supreme physical and emotional efforts put forth in this life. The feeling of giving up and being out of control compels her to say things she otherwise would not ever say. Handling what's happening to her in the same way she has been is not an option, and there is the obvious need to proceed in some kind of alternate manner.

There are a lot of similarities between birth and death. Both are such an indescribable shock to the human system. Both are out of our control, yet nothing trumps the human effort required for either. Both are unparalleled in enormity and intensity.

After my obstetrician decided to move forward with the C-section, I was wheeled into emergency surgery. My husband was sitting on my right, holding my outstretched hand that had been placed on a long board to receive an IV. The anesthesiologist was behind me, focused and quietly doing what those types of special people do so well. Something was given to numb the incision area, and as the doctor continued, I noticed the touch of someone cradling my left hand and giving it a gentle squeeze. The anesthesiologist asked me not to move my head prior to commencement of the surgery, and though I tried to glance down to see who was holding my hand, I could not see anyone.

The surgery began, but something wasn't right. I felt a sharp pain. We later found out that though uncommon, a small percentage of women feel the incision through a particular membrane that I couldn't name at this point. I was immediately under the anesthesia and woke up shortly thereafter, quite groggy but with a gift—Jennifer, our new baby girl. Later I asked Bob who had been holding my left hand, because it had given me such comfort when I was numb and so afraid. He looked at me with a question on his face and said that no one was holding it. No one. But I knew. Bob was holding my right hand, and God was there communicating His presence when I so needed Him by holding my left.

Twenty-three years later, my husband lay dying, and somehow I knew that it was time to hold his hand as he transitioned home. Our son Samuel sat on the bed next to his dad's shoulder and put his hand there. Our son Benjamin sat on the bed by his dad's side and rested his hand on his arm, and our daughter Jennifer sat on the bed near his feet and laid her hand on his leg. I was in a chair to his left, where God had been for me so many years before. Resting my hand atop each of their hands one by one as they rested theirs on his taut skin, I spoke out their names as I went and squeezed so he would know we were all there. "This is Sam, this is Ben, and this is Jenn," I told him. Then I held his left hand. He struggled, but Ben, our youngest, only thirteen at the time, said, "No, Dad. Don't struggle anymore. You've fought so long and hard." Love and pain were thick in the room, and he was gone. Samuel began to sing, and we joined him:

I love You, Lord
And I lift my voice
To worship You
Oh, my soul, rejoice!
Take joy, my King,
In what You hear
Let it be a sweet, sweet sound in Your ear.

Years ago I envisioned the Lord's hand extending to me as He gave, and I saw that it was the same hand, the same motion, with which He took. It is one and the same. When He takes, He is giving. Today as you hurt and sing your song of pain and praise, it is His kind hand that extends to you and gives. It is His gentle hand that rests on your grief and the taut skin of your emotions and heals.

Behold, the Lord's hand is not shortened that it cannot save; neither his ear heavy that it cannot hear.
Isaiah 59:1 KJV

Nine

The Unknown

ndiana Jones's quest for the Holy Grail had now become personal. His father was a victim of a shooting and awaited the healing water he hoped would be poured out over his mortal wounds and give him life. Before he could gain possession of the Grail and the celestial water his father so desperately needed, Indy must first solve a series of riddles that would lead him through a gauntlet of tests. The final challenge obstructing his path was a bottomless chasm, dark and mockingly void of any way across. It would require a step of faith, but there was nothing to step on—nothing he could even begin to make a bridge with, or the possibility of a running jump or vault, or even hope—nothing. There was no resting on his laurels, talent, experience, friends, family, reputation, or connections. His answer was *unknown* and would remain so. There wasn't even anyone to cry with. What had been asked of him was impossible.

Forty-eight hours after the neurologist's stoic announcement of my husband's fate, the word that played over and over in my mind was *unknown*.

Lord, this is entirely unknown.

Over and over. The word was so vivid in my mind I could almost see it. I was without—just . . . without. Like Indiana Jones, what lay before us was a bottomless chasm, dark and mocking. Everything was on the line, and I had empty hands. It was without measure, unknown, blank.

The word spread quickly about Bob's illness, and the next evening while he was up the street at his men's Bible study, a car pulled into our driveway, then another car, then another, and another. Cars filled every spot and lined the street. I don't know how many came that night, but we squeezed them all into our little home. Many were crying. I called Bob, and he came home as soon as he could. The men from his Bible study came too. Weeping did endure that night, and joy was a long, long way off, but we worshipped God with our grief and asked for His healing. Our son Samuel and our friend Chris took out their guitars and ushered us to the throne of grace. I remember seeing our son Benjamin lift his hands as he sang for mercy. He was ten.

After prayer, an unexpected veil of silence fell upon the room, and I felt as though we were not done. I knew the Lord was asking for us to continue praying. We were all exhausted and it was late, but we bowed low again. Out of the silence, one of our dear friends said, "Susan, I think the Lord wanted us to pray again because there is something He wants to say. It's something He wants to say to you. He wants to tell you that He is there for you in the doorway of the unknown."

In that moment, with that pronouncement, the chasm closed. No one but the Lord knew the words of dissonance that danced in my head, and He was the only note of resolve. God had stopped His world for me, it seemed, and spoke my world back into being. If He has a specialty, it's the unknown. He was telling me that whenever something looked unknown, that would be Him, waving His banner as a reminder of the intimate knowledge He possessed about me and my grief. From then on, the unknown would be the known because it would be the signal that He was there inhabiting whatever it was I didn't see or know. It was love in a word, and it not only changed me for that season, but for my entire life to come. I have leaned on the truth of the unknown until it has become an appendage, and I live there in its gentle swathe.

Indiana Jones, in a defining moment of desperation, closed his eyes and stepped out over the abyss of the unknown and unseen and walked across. Today, Grieving Saint, close your eyes and wrap yourself up in Him. It is time to rest your soul and body from their striving and find your repose in the arms of the Unknown.

He will cover you with his feathers, and under his wings you will find refuge; his faithfulness will be your shield and rampart.

Psalm 91:4 NIV

Ten

Remember

We were nearing the end. One evening I was lying next to Bob as he rested in bed. He turned to me, held me with his gaze, and said, "Remember, always remember, I love you all so much."

His words destroyed me, but I looked at him and gave my word. It would be impossible to forget. On his gravestone are the words "We'll remember."

To remember means "to bring to mind or think of again; to keep in mind, to retain in the memory, to remain aware of; or to treasure or hold dear." It implies a bringing back to mind what is lost or scattered. Its synonym, *recall*, suggests an effort to bring back to mind and often to re-create in speech.

The word's definition is highlighted when we place it next to the meaning of *forget*, which mournfully tells us to "lose the remembrance of; to treat with inattention; to disregard or overlook." Forget means "to give up hope for or expectation of; to cease noticing or to neglect; or to leave behind." To forget a person is to not have the idea of them in your conscious memory anymore. It is to ignore, abandon, dismiss, disregard, leave, or reject. According to the Hebrew, forgetting a person is even more serious than that. It means to annihilate them, to obliterate or destroy them. When God's beloved Israelites asked Him not to forget them, they weren't just requesting He think about them once in a while; they didn't want Him to annihilate them and blot them out completely.

According to theology professor Victor Shepherd, to "remember" Hebraically "is to bring up a past event into the present so that what happened back then continues to happen right now. What unfolded back then, altering forever those whom it touched, continues to be operative now, altering those who 'remember' it now."[4]

To remember is sacred. Remembering labors in seasons of grief and bears different kinds of fruit. It makes its requests amid desperation, loneliness, or intense pain. The thief on the cross petitioned Jesus to remember him moments before his death; Jesus charged His disciples at the Last Supper to partake of communion in commemoration until He came again; and my husband craved the assurance of remembrance shortly before he died. Countless others have said "remember me," so many wish they would have, and others hope to live in such a way as to garner its honor.

Truth gives you and me permission to remember. It is a holy portion of grief's work in a life. May it bear good fruit for you and give wisdom when the time comes for its pruning. For now, remember, always remember, He loves you so much.

Eleven

The Promise

I t was the nineties, and our son Samuel was just little then, maybe eight or nine. As I write, I don't know if he remembers the scene in the living room, but I know for sure his dad's death was not in this young boy's planned horizon of dreams.

Bob had just gotten home from a Promise Keepers conference, full of the present and future all at once. He had the future in sight and had always been a man of promise, but that day he made a promise he could not keep. He told us a true story he had heard during one of the sessions. The details for me are hazy, but it was something about a massive earthquake and a dad who had promised his son that no matter what happened or where they were, he would always come for him. He would find him if he was lost or hurt or scared or ashamed. The boy remembered his father's words—and so did his father. The two were separated at the time of the quake, but though the young son was trapped under piles of rubble in the aftermath, the promise gave him hope and kept him alive. His father would come as soon as he could. He would find him. He would rescue him.

For others who had been searching for survivors, hope was gone, and the desperate groping that accompanies desperate loss put the gavel down.

After days of searching and with insanity at the patriarch's heel, hope breathed life into its promise and rewarded the oath between father and son. The father found his son, and both would live now. They would live to tell their story.

That day in our living room, when Samuel was so small, his dad stood up and looked at his son and made a promise. He swore he would always come for him. No matter the cost, no matter what stood in his way, he would come. He would find his son and rescue him.

But Bob died, and I hoped Samuel would not remember that day in our living room.

Long after Bob had left us, but still floating in the wake of grief, I was wracked with other sorts of life maladies and bent over with existing. God reminded me to do what He had always taught: to come. I told Him of my weighted soul and that for the first time I could not get to Him. It felt impossible.

He said, "If you cannot make it, it's because I want you to see that I will always come for you."

And then He scooped me up. He scooped me up and reminded me of a few things:

Brothers and sisters, [I] do not want you to be uninformed about those who sleep in death, so that you do not grieve like the rest of mankind, who have no hope.[5] For since we believe that Jesus died and was raised to life again, we also believe that when Jesus returns, God will bring back with him the believers who have died. We tell you this directly from the Lord: We who are still living when the Lord returns will not meet him ahead of those who have died. For the Lord himself will come down from heaven with a commanding shout, with the voice of the archangel, and with the trumpet of God. First, the Christians who have died will rise from their graves. Then, together with them, we who are still alive and remain on the earth will be caught up in the clouds to meet the Lord in the air. Then we will be with the Lord forever. So encourage each other with these words.[6]

Don't let your hearts be troubled. Trust in God, and trust also in me. There is more than enough room in my Father's home. If this were not so, would I have told you that I am going to prepare a place for you? When everything is ready, I will come and get you, so that you will always be with me where I am.[7]

But let me reveal to you a wonderful secret. We will not all die, but will be transformed! It will happen in a moment, in the blink of an eye, when the last trumpet is blown. For when the trumpet sounds, those who have died will be raised to live forever.[8]

And he will send out his angels with the mighty blast of a trumpet, and they will gather his chosen ones from all over the world—from the farthest ends of the earth and heaven.[9]

Then, when our dying bodies have been transformed into bodies that will never die, this Scripture will be fulfilled: "Death is swallowed up in victory. O death, where is your victory? O death, where is your sting?" For sin is the sting that results in death, and the law gives sin its power. But thank God! He gives us victory over sin and death through our Lord Jesus Christ.[10]

For our citizenship is in heaven, from which also we eagerly wait for a Savior, the Lord Jesus Christ.[11]

Bob will keep his promise after all. So will the Lord. They'll come back, together. Nothing will stop them, and we'll all live to tell the story. A father will come for his son, and the Son will come for His bride. On that day, all things will be restored. For now, Believer, breathe and look up; the promise will be kept. The sting of death? I don't think so.

Twelve

Lacy

It is the horse's gift to connect us with heaven and our own footsteps.

Ronni Sweet

I held her head in my arms and leaned over to kiss her cheek. Her eyes were large and brown, soft and trusting . . . but she was confused. Learning to trust had taken a long time. We had become friends, but the possibility of reverting back to old fears and suspicions was always close to the surface. R. W. Leo Lacy lay there on her side in the wet January grass. It was cold and gray, and we had covered her with a big blanket. The four legs that had carried me for so many years could not move now; they were paralyzed, and for a horse, that was fatal. I knew when the vet called. I could hear it in his voice.

Horses were just always a part of life for me. Riding lessons when I was a kid led to owning one, then two, then three. Majesty is built into horses. Winston Churchill said, "There's something about the outside of a horse that's good for the inside of a man." But sometimes there is something inside a man that isn't so good for a horse.

When I first saw Lacy, somebody else owned her. The name *Lacy* explained her entirely. Quality bloodlines showed in every fiber of muscle and movement. She was bred for a purpose, exuded confidence, was athletic and strong, and had a sharp mind and big heart. Lacy garnered attention even as she dozed in some shade and swatted flies with her tail.

A few years later, when the owners went through a divorce, the horses were to be sold. When a call came from the woman who owned Lacy, I listened to her distress and asked the proverbial question: "How much?" The price was remarkably low for a horse of that quality, but after listening to the story, I understood why: the horses had to be sold quickly. There was a small amount in my savings, and after talking it over with Bob and calling my dad to see if he would loan me the remainder, it was done. I would pick Lacy up the next day.

It was difficult to accept what I saw when I got there. Unrecognizably thin and barely able to walk, Lacy had scabbed-over gashes on her chest, and dried blood on both of her sides told me a story I did not want to know.

After the divorce, Lacy's owner had taken the horses to another stable, where she boarded them until they all had new homes. There was a man working there who said he was an expert with horses—a "trainer." He was a fake, but Lacy's owner was weak from life and didn't stop him from inflicting harm on the horses. Lacy's spirit and ability were too much for the man to handle, so her beauty and potential became the target of his bitterness, and when she did not obey, she suffered the consequence for not performing. The "expert" said that Lacy would never amount to anything more than useless. She could never measure up to a standard he did not possess. His ignorance boasted, saying he had her hooves cut to the quick because she was "out of control." The pain of doing such a thing to a horse is incalculable. The "trainer" then got on her back and rode, wrapping his legs around her chest and digging in with his spurs until there was blood. She was in a perpetual state of fear, and the only time she partially relaxed was when she was alone.

I gave them their money, got Lacy into the trailer, and left as quickly as I could.

We returned home, and she was safe. The difficulty now was getting her to believe and trust. It was months before I could touch her face without a reaction of panic, and even longer before I could climb onto her back. True love is patient, but it doesn't sit around doing nothing. That's why Jesus came for us. So I kept on loving Lacy. I could see her potential and had great hope for her future. After a year of developing trust, she began to blossom and show glimmers of her capacity. I trained alongside a man who actually *was* a trainer and a world champion. He said Lacy was blessed with all that a pedigree could promise.

We decided to stable her at his facilities, where I could train with him regularly to get Lacy ready to show, but the day after I left her there, he called and said she was not eating. I went immediately. She was in a stall, pacing back and forth, foaming with sweat. She hated being enclosed. I think she still needed a "way out." Fear roots itself deeply. We tried a few different tactics, but after a couple of days, a cough had developed and Lacy still hadn't eaten, so we brought her home. She ate right away, and after a few days on antibiotics she was well again. In her heart, there was safety only at home, where there was no threat and no walls to challenge or constrain her. It would be so for the rest of her life, and because of it, I was never able to take her anywhere outside the boundaries of trust. Her career was over before it began, and the fulfillment of a birthright was lost.

That last winter was a bad one, and because of Bob's illness, I was not able to take care of Lacy the way I usually did. She was afraid to stay inside a stall where it was dry and would stand outside during storms, getting pelted with whatever nature threw. In years past, I had put her halter on and would lead her inside a stall where she was forced to stand, but the moment I let go, she would bolt outside. Instead of safety, she chose the elements that were against her. Everything needed for survival—food, water, and warmth—were available, but she would not trust—not even if it saved her life.

There should be more to write about Lacy, but her story ended that day on the January grass. Because of fear from the past, she would not stay in a stall where it was dry and where all her needs would be provided. An abscess developed in one of her hooves from standing in the heavy rains, and though I normally would have treated it myself, I could not leave Bob alone to tend to her. If an infection like that is not managed well, a horse can die, so a friend trailered Lacy to the vet, where they cut open the abscess, allowing it to drain. They replaced a poultice twice each day to draw out the poisonous inflammation and gave her medication for the pain and infection. Lacy had to be put into a small chute inside a large barn where she could not move during treatment. That morning, her past overcame her future. Rearing up to get away from ghosts, she hit her head on the top of the chute and fell upside down, landing on her back. The force of it paralyzed all four of her legs.

By the time I arrived, they had pulled Lacy outside with a harness in hopes of calming her. That's where I found her, and where I sat and said good-bye.

Dear Reader, you have sat beside death and said good-bye too. I do not know the circumstance of it all, whether it was due to your husband's choice or illness or injustice, but I know it is right that you grieve such a deep and desperate loss—and grieve it as hard as you can for as long as you must.

You are asking why, but it is asked in hope. You may not sense the presence of it now, but God's Word says that hope abides; it is there in you. In the midst of your January is the anchor of your soul, and He is near to you. Stay inside His love where everything you need for healing is within reach. Even though your heart has been thrown backwards and tells you to run, your provision is in Christ. He is safety and warmth. Do not stand outside His comfort where the rains will infect you with fear. He is the Balm of Gilead that draws out the abscess and pain of your loss and heals. He is the Balm of Gilead who makes the wounded whole. Do not look elsewhere to false comforts where "temporary" is the counterfeit goal.

> *I saw heaven standing open and there before me was a white horse, whose rider is called Faithful and True. With justice he judges and makes war. His eyes are like blazing fire, and on his head are many crowns. He has a name written on him that no one but he himself knows. He is dressed in a robe dipped in blood, and his name is the Word of God. The armies of heaven were following him, riding on white horses and dressed in fine linen, white and clean.*
>
> Revelation 19:11–14 NIV

Thirteen

Lost and Found

For there is nothing lost, but may be found, if sought.
Edmund Spenser, *The Faerie Queene*

Sometimes grief feels like it has a chokehold around your neck, and sometimes it feels like you will be its next victim if there is no intervention. Breathing becomes labored under the pressure of pain, and in the midst of it, you may now realize that you do not know the Christ spoken of in the pages of this book. Whether you know Him or not, it's good that you're here, and I'm glad to be here with you. If you don't know Jesus, today may be the day of your salvation.

Every morning the sun arrives through the east window of our home. I can look at it from across the room and wish I were standing inside the warmth of its rays, or I can go over and stand directly inside its warmth and receive its benefits. That's how it is with the Lord. You can look but never take the step of faith into believing and receiving His gift of forgiveness, salvation, and provision.

Think of it like this: In the Old Testament, we're told the story of Joseph, sold into slavery by his brothers because they were jealous of his integrity and their father's favoritism towards him. After surviving years of suffering and unjust imprisonment in Egypt, he miraculously became Pharaoh's right-hand man. Joseph was gifted and interpreted Pharaoh's dream, revealing the seven-year worldwide famine that was to come and advising him to store up enough provision to carry his people through the drought. When food became scarce, Joseph's father sent his sons to Egypt to buy grain from Pharaoh. None of them knew Joseph was still alive and didn't recognize him when they approached to buy their supply of food, but Joseph recognized them and overheard the brothers speaking to one another about what they had done to him years before.

Their penitence was deep and heartfelt, and Joseph was so moved "he turned himself about from them and wept" (Genesis 42:24 KJV). It soon became apparent that Joseph's love for his brothers was unconditional, and his forgiveness was free. The wrongs inflicted were reprehensible, but Joseph fell on their necks, kissed them, and reconciled them to himself.

Joseph's reaction mirrors God's heart toward us. The Bible says, "While we were enemies, we were reconciled to God by the death of his Son" (Romans 5:10 NIV). God has removed every barrier that could ever keep us from being reconciled to Him through the sacrifice of His Son Jesus on the cross, and He yearns to reveal His heart to those He loves. Reader, that means you!

Joseph told his brothers to draw near and then exhorted them not to be angry with themselves, for God had sent him to Egypt to preserve their lives. It was all a matter of unearned love. The same is true for you and me. The Bible says, "He who did not withhold or spare even His own Son but gave Him up for us all, will He not also with Him freely and graciously give us all other things?" (Romans 8:32 AMP). Joseph not only forgave but made provision for everything his father, brothers, and their families needed, including positions of favor in their work and some of the best portions of land in Egypt.

Seventeen years passed, and when Joseph's father died, the state of the brothers' hearts became evident once again. Since their father was gone, they decided Joseph would surely now express his concealed hate and pay them back for the evil they had done years before. They even sent someone else to request Joseph's forgiveness instead of asking for themselves. Seventeen years after Joseph bestowed forgiveness and offered reconciliation, the brothers remained enslaved to a lie. They misjudged Joseph's character and never truly accepted the offer of love and forgiveness. His heart was grieved because the ones he loved without measure had lived behind a veil of fear instead of living in freedom.

When Joseph found out, he wept again, but his next words would change lives forever. What the brothers meant for evil, God meant for good—for the purpose of preserving life, not taking it. He told them not to fear. He spoke kindly and promised he would always provide for them and their children, and he did.

God is saying the same to you today, Dear Reader. Do not misjudge His character. His offer of forgiveness and freedom from the burdens that chain you is free. He does not hold grudges. He wants to preserve your life, eternally.

Friend, whether you are a believer or not, you have suffered a great loss, but you need not *be* lost. You have been washed ashore. The storm has beaten you against the rocks, and you are ragged from it all, but now His embrace shines through the window and invites you this day to stand in its warmth. There is life in you yet, though you may not feel the worth of living it right now.

Here is the offer:

My Child, feel Me sweep you up off the shore and cradle your broken heart and body and soul. You are soaked through and through. I feel the heaviness of where you have been, out in the middle of the sea with no land in sight, and where you gave in to the pull of the waters. I know. Your strength was gone. But the waters did not pull you under. I have brought you here, and I will keep you. I promise. I have saved you. My Child, I have found you. You swam against the current, away from My care, away from the safety of the harbor. I heard your cry, and I know you were so afraid, but I have sought you out and found you. I have come for you, and the waters will not pull you back. It was dark and cold, but I have pulled you out. I have lifted you from the water's deep. I have brought you ashore. Your limbs are too tired to struggle against My love anymore. Be still. Hear Me breathe, but before you sleep here in My arms, say yes. Say yes to forgiveness and hope and healing. Whisper it. I can hear you. I will do the rest.

And by the way, Believer, if you were hoping He was speaking to you too, He was. Come back. Say yes to forgiveness and hope and healing. Whisper it. He can hear you too. He will do the rest. You see, there is nothing lost that cannot be found, if sought.

Fourteen

Shoulders

When Jennifer was little, we didn't notice the width of her shoulders much, but a lot of people noticed the width of her dad's. They were so unusually broad for his size that it was difficult finding shirts that fit right. What I noticed most about his shoulders was that they often carried Jennifer. As soon as she was old enough, Bob vaulted her up every chance he got. What a view. It must be a "dad thing." He carried her in the market, at SeaWorld, at Disneyland, in the mall, and everywhere in between. I remember he carried her up a mountain trail on his shoulders once to see a waterfall in Yosemite. He carried her up and over the mountainous joys and sorrows of life, and he carried her in prayer. His shoulders were broad, steady, strong, and safe.

As Jennifer got older and the expanse of life broadened, so did her shoulders. They were unusually broad for her size, and yes, it became more and more difficult to find shirts that fit right. She had her dad's shoulders. Girls don't usually have such broad shoulders, but God knew the weight of what she would need to carry as time went on.

First Corinthians 12 describes the different gifts, talents, and traits God bestows on the body of Christ with a sweeping brushstroke of color and purpose: "The way God designed our bodies is a model for understanding our lives together as a church; every part dependent on every other part, the parts we mention and the parts we don't, the parts we see and the parts we don't. If one part hurts, every other part is involved in the hurt, and in the healing. If one part flourishes, every other part enters into the exuberance" (1 Corinthians 12:24-26, The Message).

Science still doesn't fully grasp how genes and environment interact. Blind family members who participated in genetic studies were confirmed to have smiled, grimaced, and scowled like their relatives. Twins separated at birth and then reunited have the same taste in food and color preference.[12] The facts about the traits we inherit are a part of God's mysterious plan, but the night before Bob died, a small portion of the mystery unfolded. Broad shoulders aren't the only trait that Jennifer inherited from her dad, but after all the years of Bob carrying her, it seemed to be her turn to do the carrying.

Hospice had been in and out for the last week or so, and grief just kept twisting our arms behind our backs. I don't remember how long it had been since I ventured outside the house, but I know those last few weeks were spent there in our little navy- blue and white bedroom with Bob. The kids took care of each other, Rudy our pug took care of them, and friends brought meals. The pressure was something of another world, and as earthly life wept, the bleeding of our hearts began to mingle with eternity and hovered in a strange vapor. There was no song to be heard, just the rhythm of waiting . . . and life held its breath.

Darkness had fallen, outside and in, and I couldn't seem to comfort Bob anymore. He was agitated and mumbling but unable to communicate, and though his limbs had withered and become almost useless over those four years, I knew he was trying to run. He was trying to live and die all at the same time. His skin was hot, so I put a cool damp cloth on his forehead and face, but he moved his head away from my touch.

At some point that evening, my best friend Carla had arrived. I found her on the floor of the hall, propped in the doorway of Ben's room with her head bowed in her hands and praying. I knelt down next to her and noticed my face felt hot too. The cloth was in my hands, useless. Jennifer came and knelt down next to me for a moment and then quietly lifted the damp cloth and its burden from my hands and went in to comfort her dad. Later she said that he resisted her efforts too, but she stroked his head and spoke to him anyway. She told him that it was she, that it was okay, and that he should be still. So he quieted down and fell asleep for most of the night. It would be his last.

Hearing the story, I thought that when Bob heard her voice and realized it was his girl, he let her carry him and simply did as she asked. He must have relinquished control as an act of kindness. I thought it for years after his death, but as time passed, the fullness of our inheritance became clear to me. Bob had inherited *his* Father's shoulders, and even to the end, in the chasm between life and death, the inheritance allowed him to carry what no one else could shoulder.

In the same way, we could never carry our Savior's burden of love. Our sin, grief, pain, and sorrow were only His to bear. History's onlookers could not know the measure of it then, and Jennifer and I did not know the measure of Bob's sacrifice that night. He put himself aside when life and death were facing off. He said no to himself for her. He would not allow her to carry the burden and said no to demanding life so he could relieve her of the pain of watching him struggle. Even in death, she would not carry him, because where human depravity usually reigns, the Spirit of the living Christ enabled a dad to sacrifice the violently sacred human drive against death.

Bob became Jennifer's burden-bearer one last time. He was her dad even as he died. He did insist on life: her life. She was spared the agony of not being able to comfort him. He swung her up on his shoulders because somehow they were, even then, broad, steady, strong, and safe. What a view. She saw him in peace on the last night of his life; it was her reward. Jennifer denied herself by willingly facing what no child should ever have to face, and Bob's reward came in knowing that his daughter had inherited her Father's shoulders. No wonder he slept peacefully that night.

Reader and Friend, I do not know your circumstance or in what manner your husband's life was lost. I can assure you there were many times during my husband's illness when he was far from courageous and anything but steady, as was the case with the rest of us. The point is the inheritance: Jesus put Himself aside when life and death were facing off. He said no to Himself for you because He would not allow you to carry a burden that only He could shoulder; it would have killed you. Even in His death, His humanity would not reign because the love of the Father enabled Him to sacrifice His life for yours. He insisted on life: your life. Christ became your burden-bearer. When you were lost, or now as you feel lost, He has vaulted you up onto His shoulders like a lost sheep and carries you. You are His reward. His shoulders are broad, steady, strong, and safe.

Life has changed for you and your family. The expanse of it has broadened, but so have your shoulders. Go have a look in the mirror to make sure, but it looks to me like you have inherited *your* Father's shoulders after all, and that's not a bad trait to have.

> *For a child will be born to us, a son will be given to us; and the government will rest on His shoulders; and His name will be called Wonderful Counselor, Mighty God, Eternal Father, Prince of Peace.*
> Isaiah 9:6 NASB

All praise to God, the Father of our Lord Jesus Christ. It is by his great mercy that we have been born again, because God raised Jesus Christ from the dead. Now we live with great expectation, and we have a priceless inheritance—an inheritance that is kept in heaven for you, pure and undefiled, beyond the reach of change and decay. And through your faith, God is protecting you by his power until you receive this salvation, which is ready to be revealed on the last day for all to see.

1 Peter 1:3-5 NLT

Fifteen

Dancing with Your Eyes Closed

She decided to free herself, dance into the wind, create a new language. And birds fluttered around her, writing "yes" in the sky.

Monique Duvall

Carla's mom Desiré says we're all dancers inside. I have to agree. There's something of a sacred yearning to flow, swing, and sway hidden and waiting in the human heart, ever watching for an opportunity that is seldom taken. Though the depravity of man and efforts of Satan have distorted and tainted its purity, dance has been a vessel used in various cultures and eras to inspire the ones who dare, directly and indirectly, to take its hand in theirs and dance within its frame. Dance expresses emotion and often tells a story. In nature, dance facilitates a sort of nonverbal communication between protagonists. From folk dance to ballet to synchronized swimming, dance moves the emotions of its participants and audience to join in.

Some dance movements are insignificant in themselves, while others are specific and symbolic. My traditional "dance of the housewife" has survived years of scrutiny from my family, though it is done within the solitude and safety of my house, music blaring, when no one else is around. I consider the dance a sacred act of worship and champion its cause and outcome: a clean house. I don't know what the neighbors thought, but I felt as though being a widow allowed me a certain amount of impunity.

Life and death burgeon with paradox: "Blessed are those who mourn, for they shall be comforted" (Matthew 5:4 ESV). Whether those words of Jesus address a penitent sinner grieving their sin or encourage those who have lost a loved one, I'd rather just be comforted without the grieving part. That said, there cannot be one without the other, and the promise of comfort propels the open-wounded to take the hand of Jesus, follow His lead, and dance within His frame.

About a year after Bob died, somewhere inside my grief, a small, joyful commotion stirred that rhythmically whispered, "Dance." Not the housewife dance, but the "take a real lesson" type of dance. The neighbors would never have to know. I had some dear friends whose son Josh was a professional dancer, gave lessons and, amidst the pressures of the world, maintained his integrity in Christ, so I called him.

We met at the studio, where the walls were mirrored and mostly unassuming except for the twinkle lights someone had strung along one side. I began learning to dance and continued to "begin" learning, because even after three years of lessons, the moment I mastered one small angle or arch of movement, there was another angle or arch waiting to remind me of the ongoing struggle to achieve what seemed like pinky-sized victories. But with each small victory, I came closer and closer to knowing how to follow. I stumbled less and learned how to listen to Josh's almost intangible signals of movement and direction. Pretty soon I was feeling confident, and the awkwardness that had previously accompanied each step was now smooth and comfortable. I would even say I found comfort in each success.

If I tried to move in a direction other than where I was being led, of course we would get nowhere. On one such day, after my efforts of control nearly launched me into dance purgatory, Josh stopped, looked at me with his typically quizzical warmth and whimsy, and said, "Okay, but next time *I* get to lead."

We both laughed, I with a red face, and then as I took his hand and framed myself into his lead once again, he told me to close my eyes.

Much can be speculated about what happens to a person's senses when one of them is eliminated. Scientists aren't completely certain how the other senses rise to the occasion. Theory suggests when one modality of sensory input is repressed, such as sight, the others, being connected like a web, free the rest of the brain's sensory cortices to process the information.[13]

As I quickly contemplated all potential outcomes of dancing with my eyes closed, I could only hope the theories were true.

After a fruitless amount of protest, I closed my eyes and focused on nothing but the leader of my temporary destiny. The biggest decision to be made was whether I would trust him or not. There was nothing else to determine. Everything depended on it. All other information became superfluous and faded, though I did catch myself trying to cheat and open my eyes, but then immediately our movements became stiff with the interruption. I ended up more in the dark with my eyes open than I was with them closed. Trying to transition from allowing him entire control back to my pride and mistrust having their way just exaggerated my inability. Even knowing the boundaries of the dance floor became a hindrance, and the immediate necessity was not to take any responsibility for my steps except for listening to the lead. Other senses became hyperaware, and I remember smiling at the wonder of getting out of my own way. The greater my abandon, the easier the movement. The strain of self-effort melted warmly away . . . and we danced. I just relaxed into trust's frame . . . and danced.

There was comfort to be found in following each step of grief too. It was true. I not only became confident in my role as the follower, but also became confident in the one doing the leading. With that confidence came a sort of relaxing—an inner stillness and a letting go of my own agenda.

There is another paradox I never fully understood until the day I danced there in that unassuming studio with the mirrored walls and twinkle lights. David speaks of the contradiction in Psalm 30:11–12 (AMP): "You have turned my mourning into dancing for me; You have put off my sackcloth and girded me with gladness. To the end that my tongue and my heart and everything glorious within me may sing praise to You and not be silent. O Lord my God, I will give thanks to You forever."

Maybe we tend to close our eyes when we pray for the same reason. With our eyes closed, we get to gaze into the warm, quizzical whimsy of our Savior's face in a way we couldn't see if our eyes were open. His hand will lead as we step into the frame of His trust, and as we bow our senses to the sway and swing and flow of His purpose, and as the paradoxes of grief and comfort, mourning and dancing become clear, then cutting a rug and busting a move make sense in the midst of it all. Go ahead; you've earned it. The neighbors will never have to know, and in the immortal words of Mr. Miyagi (*The Karate Kid*), remember: "Never trust a spiritual leader who cannot dance."

Sixteen

The Kiss of Worship

anthropologists are divided regarding the history of the kiss. While most say it is instinctual and intuitive, one theory states that kissing evolved from an animal mother's practice of passing chewed food along to her infant's mouth. I think I prefer the first conjecture.

A kiss is a universal but diverse expression of loyalty, affection, compassion, joy, or sadness offered to another with varying degrees of intensity ranging from the gentle warmth of family and friend to intense passion or profound sorrow.[14] The earliest-known written reference to kissing is found in the Old Testament in the Song of Songs. Early Romans helped spread the expression of the kiss to other parts of the world and were said to be very passionate about the whole thing. The kiss was not only a signpost of love between a man and a woman, but could also indicate respect and rank.

As time went on, different cultures developed various versions of the kiss according to its use and meaning. In the Middle Ages, the traditional kiss indicated refinement and upper class society, but for others, a kiss was observed by rubbing one's nose on the cheek of another. Most of us have seen or heard of an athlete blowing a kiss after a touchdown, home run, or when breaking the tape in a track meet. Sometimes it's preceded by a pound to the chest, meaning the gesture is from the heart. To whom the kiss is directed is not always certain, but it's delivered toward someone, usually up.

A kiss from the right person can even wake a sleeping princess or restore a beast back into the prince he was before the casting of an evil spell. Researchers have found that kissing between married couples reduces stress, lowers cholesterol, and can burn two to three calories a minute. In ancient times, some thought a kiss bestowed upon one who had died would accompany him into eternity.

In the Greek, God's unambiguous words become invitations to a banquet of wonder. The Greek word for *worship* means "to kiss; to kiss the hand towards one in token of reverence."

Old and New Testament examples of worship tell us plainly that besides kissing, worship involves a sacrifice that is to be offered daily. If I understand that correctly, worship is a daily, sacrificial kiss—quite a combination. For the believer, worship is accompanied by faith—David or Goliath size. Rightful worship proclaims truth, burgeons through circumstances, and flowers from a *grateful heart*. Herein is the key: *gratitude*. John Piper says, "The emotion of gratitude generally rises in direct proportion to how undeserved a gift is."[15] Gratitude cannot be coerced into a person, nor is it an act of the will, nor can it be earned. *Merriam-Webster's* tells us our English word *grateful* is "a state of being." In Greek, the word for *grace* comes from the root word *charis,* and also in Greek, the word for *gratitude* is *eucharistia*. Look in the middle of *eucharistia* and you see *charis*. Look in the middle of *gratitude* and you see *grace*.

That's why gratitude can survive in the midst of your hurricane. When every emotion has been blown into shards and lies splintered on the floor of your grief, gratitude endures because it is a provision of grace and a buffer of pain. Gratitude survives the onslaught of loss and thrives in grief because it acknowledges need and admits emptiness and the inability to fill one's own abyss with hope or healing or life. It is the plea of a mysterious type of worship manifested in holy confession toward the Writer of all languages. Gratitude is the gesture of a heart swollen with strain, accepting the certainty that "grace pours its fullness into our emptiness; what we do not have is supplied by what He has."[16]

Every day during the last two years of Bob's illness, I sat in the little stuffed chair in the corner of our room, watching him breathe while he slept. It was an act of worshipping God. After Bob died, I sat in the same chair and worshipped. I sat there holding his uniform and slid my arms through the empty sleeves of fabric, pretending he was holding me. The wool was a little scratchy, but it was the fabric of a husband's love. I cried in his arms and worshipped God.

I am wordlessly grateful and thank the Lord for Bob's life. I have never thanked Him for his death, but I can still say I'm grateful because of the gift of grace. As believers, gratitude is our *state of being*. We live in the loving fabric of its embrace in the daily sacrifice of grief, and our swollen hearts continually receive fullness in our emptiness. Beloved Soul, just as grace is in the middle of gratitude, Christ is in the middle of your grief. Worship Him, and offer Him a broken and breathless kiss of gratitude. His grace upholds you. His sovereignty sustains you. The storm will not endure. Cry in the arms of His care where you are safe.

The Lord has His way in the whirlwind and in the storm,
and the clouds are the dust of His feet.
Nahum 1:3 NKJV

Seventeen

Reconstruction

Surgery is typically an intervention. A surgical procedure involves cutting tissue to fix what was torn or diseased and is considered invasive. It can be elective or emergency in varying degrees. Surgery can explore or confirm suspicions, take out an organ and put a new one in, or reattach what was severed. It has different outcomes depending on if it's an "ectomy," "otomy," "oscopy," or "ostomy."

Having kids involves ongoing interventions. Having kids in sports occasionally involves surgical intervention. Out of six possible ACLs to tear between them, my children tore five. The anterior cruciate ligament (ACL) is one of four major ligaments in the knee, responsible for its stabilization when sharp turning or high-impact planting of the leg is required. When a ligament is overloaded or experiences tension greater than it can sustain, a tear occurs. Kind of sounds like your heart right now, doesn't it?

After an injury such as an ACL tear, the body miraculously tries to heal the wound through three different phases. The *acute inflammatory stage* begins within minutes of an injury, sending blood to the compromised area. Its healing components are rich with life-stimulating purpose and even contain certain immune cells that swallow up damaging debris left over from the injury, helping form the foundation for the subsequent phase of healing.

Next, the *proliferative* or *repair phase* kicks in when the immune cells release growth factors that signal the rebuilding of ligament tissue. It's all disorganized scar tissue at this point, but the process exerts its curious benediction by depositing different kinds of protein into the mold. This arrangement courses through the body for weeks, but even though the process successfully realigns new molecules with the torn ligament, the newly formed threads are irregular.

The ensuing healing merges into the third phase of *remodeling*, often lasting for months to years post-trauma. The new tissue begins to resemble what would be called normal, but there remain critical differences in structure and function that research tells us is "grossly, microscopically, and functionally different from normal tissue."[17] In other words, the newly formed ligament tissue is inferior to the original, and because of that, what housed the old torn ligament must now become the home of something else, something unwanted at the time of injury . . . but now necessary. What was torn must be surgically removed and replaced with a new and whole ACL. Even though there are emotional, psychological, and physical variables to each individual recovery, research says that a new ACL will be stronger than the original. The knee must be reconstructed if the athlete wants to return to the same or higher levels of competition.

This is difficult to say to you, Beloved Child of God, but it is a truth that your broken heart will confirm: what housed the love of your husband must now be reconstructed. The prefix *re* means "again" or "again and again." Reconstruction will continue because He who began the work promises to complete it, and that work includes your heart's renewal and restoration. You will be rewoven and reacclimated, redirected and readapted, reaffirmed and realigned. Be assured; He will reestablish you. Again and again, God will supply the strength and fortitude to release, relinquish, and rebuild.

Surprisingly, both the heart and the ACL are considered sensory organs, meaning they give the body information about its position and surroundings. An intact or new ACL can help protect the joint and prevent injury when under stress, and it can directly or indirectly modify the load.[18] A new heart can do the same for the empty, frail spirit of loss. The heart is an extremely sensitive sensory organ that is linked to the brain and possesses its own nervous system. The heart has its own stored memories, processes meaning, and emits electromagnetic waves five thousand times more powerful than the brain that can be measured by modern instruments up to ten feet from the body.[19]

Researchers from the University of California–Davis tell us that after time, couples' hearts literally learn to beat in sync with one another.[20] "But now he's gone," you say. Your heart is torn and the rhythm has been interrupted. But I say, "It's not over."

Dear Reader, the overload and tension you are experiencing now seem greater than what the fibers of your emotions can sustain. Existence has been torn, and the shreds of all that is left hang exposed, undisguised, and unclad. There has been a rending of your soul, your courage, and your horizon. A structural change has been made, and whatever will replace the scar tissue of your brokenness must be stronger than what was there before. There could be no other answer. There could be no other way. The tear will compromise the stability of your future if left detached to heal without the Surgeon's gentle incision.

The definition of the word *widow* literally means "to be torn apart from something that you were once one with." It means "to be severed or separate." The Hebrew word for *widow* means "an empty house." The English word *void* means "empty" and originates from the same word as widow. The word can also mean "unable to speak, to be prepared apart, to be in pain, forsaken or left empty." That's why it hurts so very much.

Like an ACL, the heart of a widow cannot simply be sewn back together. No thread would hold it, and there is nothing of the old to which it can be reattached, and rightly so. The wound is ineffable. Whether a healthy marriage or not, an expected death or not, there has been a tear, and nothing short of "new" could ever repair the irreparable. If left alone to heal, stability will lose its hope, tomorrow's foundation will buckle at the slightest breeze, and emotions will crumble like last week's bread left on the counter.

Doctors and physical therapists say that shortly after ACL surgery, the new ACL temporarily becomes weaker because of the extensive healing process it must go through to fully adhere to the bones. But this is temporary. Recovery from your heartbreak will be the same. There will be weakness, but God's strength is perfected there. The foreign terrain of healing will be jagged and long, but there will be a lot of "newness" because not only are His mercies new every morning, but He also ceaselessly gives to His beloved, even in their sleep. He never tires. Never.

After ACL replacement, new blood vessels and graft material grow and develop, and a new strength slowly and agonizingly returns. There is the new pain and swelling of recovery and of beginning to put weight on the repaired limb. The same will hold true for you: new pain, swollen recovery, taking the first tenuous steps of faith. But, Dear Friend, when you walk through it all, you will not be overtaken. Believer, *you will not be overtaken*. Each moment is shaky, but that's because of the "new." Your Christ will not leave you forsaken or barren.

Following ACL surgery, a physical therapist gives his patient goals. The process is very intentional. He has a plan. Initially, the new ACL needs to be protected. Do the same for your grieving heart. Protect it. Surround it with the familiar, safe, healthy, and sacred. No major decisions, no medicating with destructive substances, no new romances, no bingeing. No. Be intentional about taking care of yourself.

The range of motion of a new ACL needs to be restored by exercising the repaired area. This is painful but necessary, balanced with rest. If the surrounding muscles are not exercised, they will atrophy and be more prone to future injury. This is your grief; it must be exercised. It must be done. Face into the work of it and you will be rewarded. There will be others—friends, family, strangers, or acquaintances—who will want or need to look away from your grief, and that's okay, but for you, remember: grief is its own comfort. Blessed are those who mourn.

> *When you pass through the waters, I will be with you; and through rivers, they shall not overwhelm you; when you walk through the fire you shall not be burned, and the flame shall not consume you.*
> Isaiah 43:2 ESV

Eighteen

Dancing in the Dark

I remember watching *The Sound of Music* when I was a child. Maria was a nun-in-training, and though her heart was there at the abbey, her ecclesiastical competency still needed some honing. She was called in to the mother superior's office to discuss her questionable future as a nun. It appeared to be God's will that as part of the honing process, Maria should be commissioned as the nanny for seven orphaned children living in a grand estate run militarily by their father, a retired captain, rigidly laid waste by the death of his wife. With resignation, Maria packed up her heart, suitcase, and guitar and ventured unknowingly into the cold grip of someone else's grief. The front doors of the mansion spanned the expanse of the entryway from floor to ceiling.

Grief does that. It becomes the new entryway into our existence and covers the expanse of our lives, floor to ceiling.

Left alone and waiting to meet the captain, Maria let her curiosity get the best of her. Along the inner perimeter of the foyer was a closed door. Maria slowly pushed the door open and went in. The room was dark—beautiful but dark. The only vestige of light came from the large ornate wall of mirrors bordering what once was meant to embrace music and dancing and celebration. There was only a reflection of what used to be—only a glimmer of the room's hope. It was obvious no one had been in the room for a long time. Maria moved into the center of the room, and then, she began to dance in the dark . . . until the captain arrived. His grief threw open the door in its anger, shattering the scene's potential and demanding center stage. Grief was wearing a uniform, standing tall and unyielding with condescension and conceit. Without words it said, "Get out!"

Our English word *grief* is derived from the Anglo-French, literally meaning "injustice, calamity, or heaviness." There are some twenty Hebrew words translated in the King James Version of the Bible as "grief," "grieve," "to be grieved," etc. Its definition can express a sense of weakness and sometimes speaks of a deep sickness in the soul. Isaiah 53:10 prophetically defined Jesus' grief as meaning to "crush Him incurably." It can mean "weariness of toil," "suffering," "pain," "bitterness," a "cause of staggering," to "faint" or "to sour"; and it sometimes implies being "bitterly or violently moved." In Psalm 73:21, "For my soul was grieved" in Hebrew means "was in ferment."

In Acts 4:2 and 16:18, the word *grief* is translated "to groan or sigh." The uses and instances of the word *grief* are notably less frequent in the New Testament, which is beautifully significant because Christ came to conquer death and comfort all who are grieving. He came to give beauty for ashes, joy for mourning, the garment of praise for a spirit of heaviness, and of course to turn our mourning into dancing.

Dear Believer, open the door, pull back the curtains, and take a step. It's a start.

Mourning makes us poor; it powerfully reminds us of our smallness. But it is precisely here, in that pain or poverty or awkwardness that the Dancer invites us to rise up and take the first steps. For in our suffering, not apart from it, Jesus enters our sadness, takes us by the hand, pulls us gently up to stand, and invites us to dance.

Henri J. M. Nouwen,
Turn My Mourning into Dancing, 2001

Nineteen

The Lamppost

It will not go out of my mind that if we pass this post and lantern, either we shall find strange adventures or else some great changes to our fortunes.

C. S. Lewis, *The Magician's Nephew*,
Chronicles of Narnia

The Smiths live on what locals call the "shady side." They are our friends and are by no means shady, but the side of the small mountain community where their home is nestled remains mostly in the shade during the winter months, thus the name. We were invited over to share Christmas Eve with them that year. It had been cold, and though California is touted as "The Golden State" because of its sunshine and poppies, the rank and file of our mountain citizens had acclimated to a mild array of seasonal fluctuations that included ice and snow. Bob was already very weakened by the disease, and "cold" was a new enemy.

He surprised Samuel with a new Taylor guitar for Christmas that night. Sam still has the guitar. It has been all over the world with him, and its sound has warmed over the years with the memory of love and the legacy of pain and healing. Today Sam leads others in worship with the same instrument that now commemorates the eternal power of a gift over the temporal power of grief, and the icy shards of that night and its approaching lament have softened and warmed over the years with the salve of music.

We left the Smiths that evening without knowing of the ice storm that had taken the way home hostage. Starting out the driveway and up the small dirt road to the paved street was quickly treacherous, and our car began to slide sideways. The street was a sheet of ice, and the possibility of travel up or down the mountain was gone. Even though we tried to maneuver back to the house, the freeze had won, and our car would have to remain in its hold for the night. All the tow trucks in the area were busy and would not be available for hours, and road conditions eliminated any thought of an emergency rescue effort.

Bob was warm in the car, but he would have to make it back to the house. The rest of us would have to grovel on hands and knees to get there safely, but for Bob to attempt the same was unthinkable. Strength and stability of frame had already been sacrificed to his illness, and the cold would slice through what muscle and skin he had left. Carrying him over the frozen glaze was not an option, and all other ideas came to abrupt ends with impossibility. I made it inside with Ben and Jennifer, and Samuel and Rich remained with Bob, devising a course of action. He could not stay where he was. There may have been temporal warmth in the car, but eventually the gas would run out and the night would not be merciful.

A decision was made and a plan unfolded. Taking the floor mats out of the car, they placed them one by one on the ice and made a path as far as the small squares would extend toward the Smiths' house. There were only two hundred yards to cover for Bob to make it to safety, but he would have to get out of the car and humiliatingly sit down on the first mat, crouching within the grasp of his son and friend, and then slowly shimmy on the seat of his pants to the next one, then to the next, and then to the next until he ended at the house. His limbs were disobedient to his masculine pride, compromising each step and movement of one who was once a stalwart firefighter and a pillar of a man. Breathing had become tenuous from the nature of the disease, and subfreezing cold would make any extended time he spent crawling from mat to mat a life-threatening risk.

Sam and Rich played hopscotch with each floor mat until the small chain of islands brought Bob to safety. By the time they got him upstairs, he was convulsing uncontrollably in cold and embarrassment, and the disease mocked him again. I held my husband in tears there in the middle of warmth and safety and friendship, but the scene wanted to hold on to its horror. I held on longer, pried the fingers of the night off of his helplessness, and warmed him up. Rich and Leah got the kids situated for the night, and the guest room became our haven of down feathers and sleep.

Years ago we were praying about some difficulty that I do not remember. What I do remember is the vision God gave and the light it has continued to shine during the darkness of life, and now death. I was in a city and it was night. The windows of the high-rise walls around me were not lit, and their stoic faces threatened any thought or attempt to move. I was standing within a small circle of light under a tall, sturdy lamppost on the corner of an empty intersection. I had no idea how I had arrived there, and no hope of direction, but I knew I needed to move. The obvious dilemma was that I couldn't see past the halo of light that encompassed what seemed to be my entire life at the moment. Then I heard the voice of one whom I knew and trusted, and He simply said, "Take a step."

My problem was that a step in any direction would land me in the total eclipse of tar-pit darkness. At least at the moment I was standing in the light. I could see through its ten-foot circumference and protect myself from the certain void that awaited.

"Take a step."

"Just let me stay here, Lord. Please." I was comforted by the familiar light.

"A step. One small step."

I did. One. I stepped off the curb . . . and the light walked with me. I don't know how, but one step lifted my other foot, and then another step followed. No matter where I walked, I was surrounded by a luminescent bracelet of light. I was still in the city and within range of its eerie peripheral taunts, but I walked within the lamppost's glow and still do.

Today you have a step to take. It may be just off a curb, or it may involve worming your way across the ice of your grief on a floor mat. Either way, the light is in you, surrounding you, going before and following behind. He conquered the grave, and He'll conquer your fear. The comfort of the "temporaries" of this world is not what you need.

Take a step. Brush your teeth today. Make the bed. Then take the next step. The light goes with you and will illuminate your way. Wash the dishes. Take plenty of time to cry. Be intentional about grieving. Plan for it; that way you can have some control over it instead of "it" controlling you. Strength and stability have been sacrificed, and each step and movement has been compromised. Life is not what it was, but it will become more. His light will pry the fingers of grief away when it is time, and you will stand instead of crawl. For now, just one step at a time, like steppingstones. Wear His bracelet of light around your heart; it is the eternal power of a gift over the temporal power of grief.

> Again Jesus spoke to them, saying, "I am the light of the world. Whoever follows me will not walk in darkness, but will have the light of life.
>
> John 8:12 ESV

The light shines in the darkness, and the darkness has not overcome it.

John 1:5 ESV

The Lord is my light and my salvation; whom shall I fear? The Lord is the stronghold of my life; of whom shall I be afraid?

Psalm 27:1 ESV

The people dwelling in darkness have seen a great light, and for those dwelling in the region and shadow of death, on them a light has dawned.

Matthew 4:16 ESV

And I will lead the blind in a way that they do not know, in paths that they have not known I will guide them. I will turn the darkness before them into light, the rough places into level ground. These are the things I do, and I do not forsake them.

Isaiah 42:16 ESV

And the city has no need of sun or moon to shine on it, for the glory of God gives it light, and its lamp is the Lamb.

Revelation 21:23 ESV

Your sun shall no more go down, nor your moon withdraw itself; for the Lord will be your everlasting light, and your days of mourning shall be ended.

Isaiah 60:20 ESV

Twenty

What's in a Name?

You are a widow now, but that is not all you are or all you ever will be. Some of your identity, including your last name given in marriage, will linger from before your husband died and the color of your world grew dim. Other dimensions of life will be exchanged, adjusted, refined, or replaced. There are sunsets of endings, but the same horizon that bids us good night will proclaim a new day tomorrow. Evening comes and morning follows, each with a name.

> *God called the light Day, and the darkness He called Night. God called the firmament Heaven.*

And God called the dry land Earth, and the gathering together of the waters called He Seas.
Genesis 1:5, 8, 10 KJV

Two days after Bob died, Jennifer and I visited the nearby mall to buy clothes to wear to his funeral. Time had been consumed with the death of his life, but it seemed the rest of life consumed itself while we were absent from it. It was just . . . gone. It was a surreal experience; my husband and the father of our three children had just died, and we were shopping in a mall, living in a murky other-world unknown to the strangers standing in line at the cashier and food court. They would never know him, and they did not care. His name was Robert. Robert Ortega. His middle name was Miranda—a family name that each of his brothers and sisters shares. It means "admirable." I wanted to stop each passerby and tell them his name and that he was gone, but while thinking about it, I noticed something: his name hadn't died.

During my training and certification in grief counseling, I learned the importance of asking the family the deceased's name, to remember it, and to use the person's name during counseling and conversation. A name is important. Very.

Cultures differ as to how a name is given. Many maintain a sense of ancestry or adhere to specific rules when considering a name. Others are sometimes christened from the result of a serendipitous event during pregnancy, or from a favorite hero or heroine portrayed in literature, or borrowed from a place or figure in the Bible. Somehow, having a name solidifies a person's existence in society and sets them apart from others. An individual becomes "known" by his name, and others associate what they know about that person with their name.

You can buy a baseball in any market or drugstore around, but if that same baseball holds the signature of a famous player, the ball immediately becomes more valuable than the price originally paid. A name validates a birth certificate, passport, driver's license, marriage certificate, and death certificate.

When Bob died, his name did not disappear from any of these documents. The same is true for your husband.

Identity theft violates the sanctity of a name and carries a hefty penalty. When convicts are taken into prison, their names are exchanged for a number—a great humiliation and consequence of what they've done. In certain sororities and fraternities, a member's name can be struck from the records with indelible ink to assure none in the future will learn of their infidelity or disloyalty, and in accordance with some military school regulations, when a cadet is disgraced, a ceremony marks their dismissal and all are warned not to utter their name again. Still, none of these actions can eliminate the fact that the person existed. God knows their name, and He knows the number of hairs on a head on any given day. More than that, He *knows us.* This "knowing" is Love's prize.

Psalm 46:10 admonishes, "Be still and know that I am God."

To *know* someone means much more than knowing their name. To truly know someone is to have a personal, intimate relationship, and it is often signified by possessing exclusive information about them. Such fathomless "knowing" runs deeper than a word or name—even deeper than what it was to be able to finish your husband's sentences, recognize his footsteps, decipher what he was thinking or feeling by the look in his eyes, or know what wounded his heart or enflamed his passions.

To *be still* means "to be weak, to let go, to release—or to let yourself be weak."

Being still involves our "surrender" in order to know that God is in control as *Ribbono shel Olam*, the Master of the universe. We "let go" to know the saving power of God in our lives. We give up trusting in ourselves and our own designs to experience the glory of God's all-sufficiency.[21]

Living in stillness means casting a burden down—to just let it fall, and then to relax. Consider the image of letting your wearied arms and hands simply hang down at your sides after transferring your boulder of a burden to another's arms. Now consider casting down the relentless impulse to take the boulder back again. This is stillness before God. Your arms are throbbing anyway, my Believing Friend. God knows you because He formed you. He knows your name . . . by heart. He calls your name now. God intentionally loves you; intentionally let Him.

With the birth of each of our children came a name. Jennifer means "tender one" or "fair one." Samuel means "answered prayer" or "asked of God." Benjamin means "son of the right hand." Each name burgeons with the personal meaning of more than can be said—especially now. Each middle name completes the sentiment begun by the first. Their last name lives on with them though its patriarch has left for heaven.

A few months before Bob died, I asked him what the first word was that came into his mind when I said "Jennifer."

"Beautiful," he replied.

"And Samuel?"

"Gifted."

"Benjamin?"

"Joyful."

I penciled the moment down on paper and still have it. I remember the venerable effort it took for him to mouth the words. I remember the watery look in the sunken eyes of a heart gazing back to a past that would end too soon. But his name still lives on. We knew him. This is Love's prize.

I also remember how the breeze stood still at the firefighter memorials when they said his name out loud and the brass bell rang out. But his name lives on in those who share it and the ones who knew him. Love's prize.

The kids and I still meet people who didn't know Bob but heard of his life of faith and about his story. "Though he is dead, yet he still speaks" (Hebrews 11:4 NASB). Love's prize.

Molded into Bob's gravestone is a heart with "Dad" in the middle, two wedding rings entwined, a firefighter badge, and a Bible with one of his favorite verses: "Blessed is the man who perseveres under trial; for once he has been approved, he will receive the crown of life which the Lord has promised to those who love Him" (James 1:12 NASB). His name is also engraved there in bronze under the breath of the pines by a little pond.

Bob has a new name now, a better one: "And I will give him a white stone, and a new name written on the stone which no one knows but he who receives it" (Revelation 2:17 NASB).

There is much more in a name than we ever imagined, but right now we see only in a dimly lit mirror. One day we will know fully, even as we have been fully known. We will be known as overcomers and pillars in the temple of God. He will write His own name on our identities and does so even now. You are His and are sealed by the Holy Spirit of promise. His name was mocked at Calvary so that you could know Him and be known as His. You are Love's prize and He is yours. Your darkest hour cannot hide Him from you. Be still and know. Drop the burden once again. He never grows weary of taking it from you. You are the daughter of the Most High, and He knows you by name.

In Jewish tradition, when the name of God is transcribed on a permanent document, the writer is never to pen all the letters because the name is ineffably sacred and the risk should never be taken that would allow for the destruction of a document that bears it. Instead, the name is written G-d, substituting a symbol for a letter.

Your husband's name carries a sort of sacredness for you, and rightly so. God understands and so do I. I'm walking through this with you, and I wanted to set aside a place for you to honor your husband. If you'd like, write his name down below and say it out loud. It will hurt, but do it anyway. It all hurts, so make it count. If anyone else ever reads your copy of this book, they'll read his name and say it out loud too. Then they'll add their husband's name. Write it here. You can write its meaning too if you like.

Be still. Know. He is God. Hold fast.

Twenty-One

Gracing

We sat facing each other, knees touching. The house was quiet and we were alone. Bob was sitting in his recliner—the one I said I'd never own. He sat there each day and every night until bedtime, but eventually he couldn't push himself up from the reclining position any longer, so I did it for him. The first time it happened, he clenched his teeth and cried in disgust and disdain at himself, at me, and at God too. He tried to pound both of his fists on the arms of the chair, and flailed his legs and body, trying to get it to move, but he lacked the strength to make much more than the sound of a few thuds.

The wilderness in him moaned, and the sound of it echoes in a recess deep inside me to this day. Soon he couldn't pull a Kleenex from the tissue box to wipe his tears, so we did it together. He was continually humiliated, and I continually tried to hide how much I loathed my failed attempts to love and serve him unconditionally, but in the hindsight of grief, I have never had a greater honor than to push up a recliner and wipe my husband's tears.

God's grace doesn't suppress sin; God's grace conquers sin, so that night, face-to-face, knees touching, I asked for its clemency. If it meant Bob's life, I would confess and ask forgiveness and even take responsibility for wrongs I had not done. The Bible says to confess sin to one another, to pray for one another and be healed. Okay. I confessed everything I could think of, trying desperately to play the bargaining hand of my fears with God. Pride cowered and was crucified that evening, and in the shadow of Love's banner, forgiveness transcended shame. We both ended up confessing sin that didn't matter and exchanged regret and failure for victory and grace. We even laughed a bit, but God didn't heal Bob. He did so much more.

Months after he left us, the kids started having friends over to the house again. They piled into the living room and filled it with warmth and friendship. I loved them all. They didn't know about the chair's sentiment, and I had no reason to divulge the fact, but I hadn't anticipated the sanctimonious inferno of anger that erupted in my gut when one of the teens plopped himself down in Bob's recliner for the first time. He leaned back and even had the nerve to hang his leg over the side. My heart railed at the violation. Someone obviously needed to explain grief etiquette to this rebel pubescent who moments earlier I had welcomed into our home with glad tidings. I walked into the other room to calm my righteous indignation and remembered the lesson of the very chair in which the young man sat. Grace.

During Bob's illness, the request for prayer was ongoing. On one such occasion, a dear sister proclaimed Bob's healing. She said we had God's favor. On a separate Sunday, another sister felt it her duty to proclaim the opposite, and on yet another day, as Bob sat in his recliner, a brother invaded the sanctuary of our home only to reveal the sacred message entrusted to him: God would not heal Bob. Grateful to finally have life all figured out, I thanked the brother and escorted him to the door. I clutched his cruelty next to my heart and placed it secretly in a little velvet sachet from which I could pull out the yellow callused thing it would grow into for future use. Long after Bob died, I saw the brother again, and though still in possession of the sachet and its contents, I remembered the lesson of the chair and felt the painful memory beneath the hardened skin of my heart heal and fade away. I emptied the pouch of its gratuitous calluses—and my shame—into the wind. God did much more than heal Bob. That's grace.

A week or so after the diagnosis, Joe and Steve came to visit their beloved friend. They had all been partners in ministry and life for many years and arrived without words and without needing any. After a few attempts at small talk, Steve fell on his face at Bob's feet and began to pray, and Joe fell to the floor beside him. I will never forget the moment. Bob was in the recliner, and the lesson of grace displayed itself there once again, but we knew of others who could not face the diagnosis. They never came or called or sent a Hallmark sentiment, yet they loved him, and we recognized their love in the weight of their absence. Others might call them cowards or self-centered, but I thought of it as a type of courage. After all, it is a strong will that says no to facing the death of a friend. We couldn't even face it ourselves, and there were days early on that I had to leave the house to escape its stare. So, we loved them all no matter what and gave up the right to have an opinion about how they dealt with Bob's illness and death. This can only be the work of grace.

Standing behind the podium at Bob's memorial service, I spoke about the gospel and about grace. I offered grace to those who could not face Bob while he was alive and assured them that I was the recipient of the same grace, as evidenced by my presence there. At the reception, an elderly man I did not know shyly came and thanked me for offering emotional impunity from the guilt that had plagued him. He loved Bob and had been a member of his Bible study but could never bring himself to face his friend's decline and mortality. The moment ended with an embrace and a nod of understanding and grace. Later I heard about one of our dearest friends who had given his life to Christ during the service that late afternoon. Bob was free, and now they were too—all because of grace. God did more than heal Bob.

Dear One, God and His grace will do so much more than heal your broken heart. John Piper says God is "always doing more than one thing." His hands are open before you today, displaying the pierced offering laid bare and unhidden as payment for your restoration and to symbolize the conquered grave of resurrection hope that is your home and solace now.

The frostbite of regret and sin are often left without resolve during grief's tempest, but God's kindness draws you under His wing of grace in the wake of unfinished apologies and lost opportunities.

I have heard it said, "The blackest of sin is not righteousness violated but mercy despised."[22] There is no wrong done by your husband or by another or by you that cannot find grace in the arms of the Father's goodness. He extends its gift to you to receive and for you in turn to extend to others. Do not neglect so great a salvation or delay your response to God's kindness. Empty your little velvet pouch of self-loathing, shortcomings, accusations, finger-pointing, and man's cruelty into the wind and live in grace.

Be ye kind to one another, tenderhearted, forgiving one another [gracing one another] even as God has forgiven you [has graced you] in Christ.
Ephesians 4:32 JUB

Or is it that you think slightingly of His infinite goodness, forbearance and patience, unaware that the goodness of God is gently drawing you to repentance?
Romans 4:2 Weymouth

When the dove was weary, she remembered the ark and flew into Noah's hand at once.
Charles Spurgeon

Twenty-Two

Treasure

I will give you the treasures of darkness and hidden wealth
of secret places, so that you may know that it is I, the Lord,
the God of Israel, who calls you by your name.
Isaiah 45:3 NASB

hroughout history, storing treasure in hidden
subterranean locations was commonplace. Treasure is
not only defined by monetary worth but, according
to archaeologists, includes anything that can tell about how
humans lived and died in the past. When an archaeologist
uncovers valuable items, he is careful to document his findings

and keep them safe. Valuables must be protected from thieves, but also from corrosion resulting from removing the item from its normal environment.

A treasure can be anything precious or valuable, including gems or metal. Treasure can be selfishly hoarded, but the better use of it is storing it up for future use to secure someone else's well-being and strength. Treasure is considered something precious or rare, something to be cherished, as a prize that one safeguards and holds dear. To treasure a person is to grasp their very nature and significance. We get our word *thesaurus* from the same Greek root word as treasure. It literally means a "deposit." In Hebrew, it means "made ready."

My Friend, the Christ of your grief gives you His treasury of wealth there in the dark of your hiding place, and what you find there is yours to keep and will be a sacred portion of a story yet to be told. Your past is not lost but will be the foundation of your future. Neither rust nor moth will destroy it because though you feel your permanent abode is now an empty shaft, you are really seated in the hollow of His hand.

You have no doubt discovered a secret place to weep. Sometimes your weeping is silent and your screaming is hidden, buried under your personal ruins. Sometimes the tears are seen, but the work of grief is done mostly in the dark amidst the rubble. From under its cover you have asked Him, "Where are You?" The Persian poet Rumi said, "The most secure place to hide a treasure of gold is in some desolate, unnoticed place. Why would anyone hide treasure in plain sight?" Such is the treasure of your grief.

A secret place is a "hiding place"[23] where the inestimable wealth of conversation and communion between Father and daughter occurs. It is here in God's storehouse of provision that He will collect your tears and archive your pain, and where He will protect and prepare you. He will not shortchange you. Your darkest night is part of His day, and your hiding place is under His shadow. The revealed treasure will help secure your well-being and strengthen you. It will profit you and your family. Your loss is your treasure, and it is His treasure as well. What you invest here in this secret place will be redeemed, and the value of the original deposit will increase and multiply into eternity. Dig deep, Believer, for where your treasure is, there will your heart be also (Luke 12:34 ESV).

Twenty-Three

The Veil

You think that their dying is the worst thing that could happen. Then they stay dead.

Donald Hall, "Distressed Haiku"

On the death of his wife, poet Jane Kenyon

I read somewhere about an old Jewish teaching based on the superstition that a person's soul hovers over their dead body for the first three days after passing in hopes of returning to its owner. Some commentaries cite this superstition as a possible reason Jesus waited until the fourth day to raise Lazarus from the dead. There is no biblical evidence for such reasoning, but I understand grief's desperation and the blind rationale of severed love.

I understand grasping. The heart demands the return of what was taken, and death isn't explanation enough. Something otherworldly stealths under the surface of grief's restraint, and sometimes the pressure of it feels like imprisoned rage and is expressed in the beating of one's breast or the tearing of one's clothes in denial. I remember times of sobbing in the dark, yanking and pulling the shirt or sweater I was wearing. If I could have torn it, I would have.

After Bob died, our dear friend and pastor Rich wanted some time alone in the room with him before the coroner arrived. He and Bob had spent countless hours together during his illness, and their love was deep. I didn't initially know what transpired during those moments, but later I found out that Rich had, with forethought, asked the God of the living and the dead to raise his friend up from the dead. He asked the Lord to give him back. Friendship's love was torn in two, and he asked that God make it right again and mend the tear.

Each day for months and months, I drove to Bob's graveside and sat on a blanket next to the cutout of grass where they had buried him. During his illness, I read to him almost every morning but never got to finish the two books we had begun, so I finished reading them out loud there by his grave. During the first week, before I started to read, I would ask a question similar to what Rich had asked:

"Lord, if You'll raise him, I'll dig him out."

Not that God couldn't tear the ground open as well as raise a person from the dead, but grief churned so violently inside that, given the chance, I would have torn the earth apart myself to get him back.

The day heaven cried and our Christ was crucified, the veil that separated the Holy Place from the Holy of Holies in the temple at Jerusalem was torn in two, top to bottom. There was no longer any separation between Jew and Gentile, and what was before only the privilege of the high priest (only one day of the year) was now the gift to all mankind. The veil was woven in varied types of thread and was the thickness of a hand's width. Its dimensions were so massive in scale and weight that it is said to have taken hundreds of priests to move it. Its tearing was of such magnitude that commentators agree no human could have torn it. The rending was a violent supernatural act of love, and the torn veil is now the opening through which we enter into His holy presence.

Some believe the rending of the veil also symbolically represents the unfathomable grief present that day in the Father's heart. Maybe His heart was the veil, and for you and me to enter the Holy of Holies, He tore His own heart open.

In God's kind irony, to be a widow is to be torn, but now the tear of loss is the same opening through which your God will make a way for you, and grief's gaping hole of poverty will be filled by His plenty. His heart was torn so that your torn heart could be healed, and the same power that tore the veil, opened the tomb, and raised Jesus will open the tomb that is your heart right now and resurrect what seems so final.

And behold, the veil of the temple was torn in two from top to bottom; and the earth shook and the rocks were split.

Matthew 27:51 NASB

Therefore, brethren, since we have confidence to enter the holy place by the blood of Jesus, by a new and living way which He inaugurated for us through the veil, that is, His flesh, and since we have a great high priest over the house of God, let us draw near with a sincere heart in full assurance of faith.

Hebrews 10:19-22 NASB

Thou hast made us for Thyself, O Lord, and our hearts are restless until they rest in Thee.

Saint Augustine

Twenty-Four

Payment

He Himself is the sacrifice that atones for our sins—
and not only our sins but the sins of all the world.
1 John 2:2 NLT

After one of Samuel's knee surgeries, his leg got infected. The whole limb was burning and swollen. The ER doctor loosened the bandages, and with the careful cutting and tearing open of skin and suture, the foul contents exploded like liquid shrapnel. The releasing of it was its own anesthetic, but the infection was severe and critical. They would perform emergency surgery and clean out the toxins. After the surgery, Samuel suffered a number of severe allergic reactions to most of the antibiotics they tried and then underwent another surgical procedure to clean out the infection again. Recovery took a long time, and now Sam bears a much larger scar than he would have had the surgery gone as planned.

Viruses and germs and disease exist, good people do bad things, and questions go unanswered. Humans are fallible and make errors in judgment or willfully do wrong. Sometimes they are ordinary people, and sometimes they are of high rank. Evil is intentional and overcomes and persuades some men to steal and kill and destroy. As a result, we all bear much larger scars than we would have had life gone as planned.

Death is an epidemic that brazenly discolors and misrepresents life. Its guile can make us cry out demanding just recompense for what has been taken. Sometimes, if we were honest, it wouldn't even matter if the recompense was unjust as long as someone paid—if someone could make it right. If only it would all fold up neatly, pressed and creased and placed in a drawer, but the violation of death seems to have no manners. The face of it shows up wherever it wants and is always in contempt of court.

Beloved Friend, there is no manmade payment that can appease your loss. There is no one with fortune enough to reimburse you for such a treasure, but blame is evil's coconspirator and will continue to steal if you insist on dealing with him. The contract must be torn up because it is a counterfeit. Whether your husband's death was at the hands of another's willing intent or accidental, neither you nor the other answers to anyone but the Lord. To blame is to dishonor and lessen the value of your loss. To blame is to take the seat of judge, and you will not do well to take on the position of the living God because then you will be the one who is stealing. You have been bought with a price; do not become the bond servant of blame. Do not sow to your flesh, because you will only reap a harvest of decay, but if you sow to the Spirit, you will reap an abundant life here and into eternity. The sacrificial Lamb was and is the atonement for sin—not only yours, but whomever you want to blame.

You and I may scream and pound our fists and insist that someone must be held responsible. Well, Jesus said He'd be the responsible party. Will you point your finger of blame at Him? You and I may still contend that someone should pay, but that's the point--Someone did.

The authorities placed here by God may require you to walk a path after your loss that will take you through legal proceedings, and of course you may do so if He leads, but before you go, release the other party in your heart; they can't pay you back any more than the infection in Sam's leg could pay for the hospital bills.

Then you shall call and the Lord will answer; you shall cry and he will say, "Here I am." If you take away the yoke from your midst, the pointing of the finger, and speaking wickedness, if you pour yourself out for the hungry and satisfy the desire of the afflicted, then shall your light rise in the darkness and your gloom be as the noonday. And the Lord will guide you continually and satisfy your desire in scorched places and make your bones strong; and you shall be like a watered garden, like a spring of water, whose waters do not fail. And your ancient ruins will be rebuilt; you shall raise up the foundations of many generations; you shall be called the repairer of the breach, the restorer of streets to dwell in.

Isaiah 58:9-12 ESV

Twenty-Five

Good Posture

d umbo's momma had been locked up, and he was left to fend for himself. She was protecting him from danger and further exploitation, and enough was enough—but then it all happened so fast. The onlookers thought she was mad, and chaos ensued. The circus tent fell that night, and the next scene reveals little Dumbo, swaying back-and-forth and all alone in the dark, ears unfettered and crying elephant-size tears.

The sackcloth of old was worn during extreme times of grief and was an outward indication of deep inner sorrow. The cloth was woven from goat's hair, coarse and black, formless and girded close around the waist and afflictive to the skin.

The to-and-fro of the weave is said to perhaps represent the to-and-fro of a grieving and restless soul, wounded and bleeding, caught and cornered, swaying back-and-forth, desperate and without escape.

We lived for many years in a lovely navy-blue house in a little canyon. The kids grew up there amidst joy and sorrow and all the back-and-forth and to-and-fro of life. Guarding the back bedrooms were two grand oak trees that shaded the brick floor and painted lumber of the pergola Bob built right before he became ill. In the winter, the canyon often ushered monstrous winds down through its hillside walls. Their tenacity ruptured the quiet cold, causing the quaking and moaning of the oaks' heavy wood. Sometimes we'd hear the thud of a branch that had given in and broken off onto the roof. It was a sight to see, watching those old trees bend and heave back-and-forth, to-and-fro.

Studies have been done to uncover the mystery of why babies love to be rocked back and forth and why just being held doesn't seem to have the same effect. Evidently, "rocking causes the nervous system to activate movement detectors within the cerebellum and prompts an involuntary response."[24] The heart instinctively slows down, and the baby calms and is able to sleep. There is also a "dramatic boosting of sleep-related brainwaves that specifically increase the duration of deep non-dreaming sleep."[25] Further investigation also evidences the fact that adults fall asleep more quickly and sleep better after being rocked to sleep too.[26]

Researchers trying to improve the success rates of in-vitro fertilization for humans have even proven that mouse embryos prefer to be rocked by simulating the rocking motion in a petri dish. Without explanation, "the embryos seem to notice."[27] Embryos grown in static conditions contained an average of 67 cells, while embryos that were rocked contained 109 cells. An embryo grown inside the body averages 144 cells.

The term *shockling* in Yiddish refers to a person's swaying back-and-forth during Jewish prayer or reading of the Torah, though there is no evidence affirming the posture's origin. I often see fellow believers sway during worship, and I have found myself doing the same.

And so it was in the City of David. The newborn Savior was swaddled and no doubt rocked back-and-forth, to-and-fro, in his momma's arms. And so it was when the Savior died— the earth rocked back-and-forth and to-and-fro as the heavens declared His glory and His grief. And so it is the good posture of a Christian to rock and sway in unfettered sorrow and woe and in worship. The fabric of mourning clothes the heartsick soul, and the everlasting arms will cradle and protect you in the back-and-forth and to-and-fro of your restless pain and cornered desperation. "Be still, my soul: the Lord is on thy side."[28]

A bruised reed He will not break.
Isaiah 42:3 NASB

Twenty-Six

Tools

as Bob's condition worsened, the home health-care truck began to make its regular deposits of tools and equipment needed to make his journey to heaven easier. In my mind, the letters on its side advertised death and were a prophetic reminder with each visit. Gratitude and abhorrence coexisted each time the truck pulled into our driveway and unloaded the contents of what seemed to be one of those recurring nightmares that never resolve.

The wheelchair ramp and wheelchair came first, then a walker, and then a chair for the shower. A raised toilet seat with handrails came with a portable toilet to sit next to his bed, and then oxygen and something to suction the phlegm from his throat. After a short while, Bob couldn't stand long enough or muster the strength he needed to shower himself, so the necessity of humility presented its gift of opportunity once again. We had only a standard showerhead, and I needed the handheld kind to wash him, so I purchased one from the local hardware store. Not yet having mastered the art of plumbing, I was reticent to try to attach it myself, so Carla's son Nathanael installed the extension and showerhead on my behalf. It will always remain one of the greatest gifts of love I have ever received. I needed to wash my husband, and the little showerhead became a daily expression and extension of love's required task.

In the garage covering much of the far wall hangs a sacred piece of plywood. Only a man would understand how such a thing could be considered sacred. On the plywood is a meticulously fashioned outline of every tool Bob owned, barring the ones requiring power. Filling each outline was the tool itself. Though we don't live there any longer, and though the tools belong to the kids now, the plywood still remains and oversees the present occupants' daily goings-on. Each tool had a specific purpose and, when in use, was an extension of the one who determined its task. When the task was complete, the tool was returned to the appropriate outline for accessibility and future use.

After Bob died, the tools fell into the hands of young imaginations and began to fulfill many new and interesting callings. Screwdrivers dug holes, hammers squashed bugs, and shovels became swords. Some of the tools were left unused for lack of knowledge or an alternative, while others were off-limits because they were dangerous in the hands of adolescent boys or because the skill to use them required a teacher's guidance—but the teacher was no longer there. When the boys would move on to a new adventure, the tools would periodically and sacrilegiously be left outside to rust or deposited on the worktable, caked with the dirt of innocent abandon.

I will admit to misusing the tools from time to time myself. Weaker than Bob and without him around, I needed the force of a hammer, vise grip, or wrench to do some damage to a household item that wouldn't obey my female wishes. Sometimes the original object of my aggression ended up being in worse shape than before the undertaking, but sometimes . . . it worked. The tools I held in my hands slowly became fluent in the new language of "widow" and were once again the extension of the one who determined their task.

Beloved Daughter of God, when your husband was here, you were the recipient and holder of a great gift. Whether your marriage was perfect or not isn't in question here because the Master is skilled in His craft of molding, shaping, chiseling, and engraving, and so imperfections are His delight. Marriage is partnering, co-laboring; agony and bliss. The tools a couple uses for the journey's success are extensions of the original vow of God and come from Him who does not change or revoke His promises of salvation, mercy, compassion, or presence (Romans 11:29). They will not be altered or undone or exchanged. What was given to you then is still yours and will now be a part of your future's equipping. All is not lost. The tools of your new trade may need to be used differently and will feel unfamiliar, but God will teach you. You will not be abandoned or left to the corrosive elements of grief.

You were once the bride of your husband, and you lived and loved beside one another, girding the other up through the trials and passions required to mold two people into one. You lived and loved under his ordained and difficult calling of authority, protection, provision, and masculinity, and he lived under your wings of service, tender sacrifice, nurturing, and cadence. Now, you are still a bride, and you are the daily expression of God's love. He continues to gird you up and equip you, and His sanctuary of authority, provision, and protection is still your home. Your Christ is fluent in the language you speak, and He has meticulously fashioned the outline of your future. Dear Friend, you are your Savior's delight and the extension of the One who holds you.

> *The one who calls you is faithful, and He will continue to be faithful.*
> 1 Thessalonians 5:24 ISV

> *For it is God who works in you to will and to act in order to fulfill His good purpose.*
> Philippians 2:13 NIV

> *This is what the Scriptures mean when they say, "No eye has seen, no ear has heard, and no mind has imagined what God has prepared for those who love Him."*
> 1 Corinthians 2:9 NLT

Your boundary lines mark out pleasant places for me.
Indeed, my inheritance is something beautiful.
Psalm 16:6 GWT

TwentySeven

Eclipse

The mind has a dumb sense of vast loss—that is all. It will take mind and memory months and possibly years to gather the details and thus learn and know the whole extent of the loss.

Mark Twain

Obstetricians go on vacation. Mine had his scheduled for around the time our second child was to be born. During the period between Jennifer's birth and this one, a miscarriage had broken our hearts, and the test results informed us that the chances of having another child were slim; but God gave a gift of life that would later eclipse death's aftermath.

Giving birth minus the necessity of a C-section was the hope, but there had been too many complications during the pregnancy, and the penciled-in due date was erased and exchanged for the twenty-fifth—our anniversary. We would have chosen another day if given the option, but a doctor's life is defined by long hours and sacrifice, and their vacation plans are not to be violated. Samuel was our anniversary gift that year and would continue to be a gift in a way we could not have foreseen. He was an answer to prayers that hadn't been spoken yet and to a need that did not yet exist. He was the only one of our three whose name we selected prior to birth. Samuel means "answered prayer" or "asked of God." Now, every year, we celebrate the answered prayer that is Samuel's life. On a day that would otherwise have been only a reminder of loss, his birth eclipsed our pain and is now a reminder of God's compassion, efficiency, and love.

God answers prayers of the moment within the bookends of past and future and reconciles the unresolved questions of what was or what could have been with what will one day be. He includes answers to inquiries that have not been made or imagined. He satisfies the prayers of the present moment with more than just the present moment's answer.

Shortly before Bob was diagnosed with Lou Gehrig's disease, the church we called home suffered a split, and the pastor we loved was forbidden to open or pastor another church by a non-compete agreement. In the interim, we visited another church close by and fell in love. The pastor became Bob's dearest companion, confidant, and encourager during his illness, and his wife Leah became a treasured friend. It was this pastor who beseeched God to raise Bob from the dead that rainy afternoon, and it was Leah's half-brother Lee, whom she had never met, who sought her out after a lifetime without Christ, got saved, and is now married to our daughter Jennifer. God answered the cry of our hearts with what we didn't know we needed and has turned the barren soil of grief into a harvest of life.

Bob looked forward to being a counselor at Hume Lake every summer. The small group of counselors from our church had become close through those years of tents and games, and late nights and worship, and though the kids who went to camp then are now grown, they still talk about the impact Mr. Bob had on their lives. So do the adults. One girl in particular stands out from amidst the memories of those summer days as a lifelong beneficiary of his influence. She is now married to our son Samuel. Her mom and dad were counselors at Hume Lake too.

Cheyene and Sam grew up together as kids in church do, lost touch as time passed, then reconnected years after Bob died. They fell in love and made plans to be married. The joy of the wedding day eclipsed the ambient pain of Bob's absence that accompanied each of us down the aisle of the occasion. There was still a subtle but deep sense that someone was missing and that we should wait just a few more minutes until he arrived, but the truth was, Bob would not be joining us in the festivities, toasts, or wedding day pictures. His presence was tangible in so many ways, but he was gone.

God, however, already answered a request that had never been made and filled a present and future need with the ordained circumstance of what had already transpired. While the romance was in its infancy and before the wedding plans had begun, Cheyene's mom came across an old photo of Bob, Chey, and her dad Steve taken together at Hume Lake. Somewhere in the midst of the tents, games, late nights, and worship of summers past, a picture was taken of what the future held: a family picture. The three who would one day be a family stood in a memory captured in time before death would have a say.

Before we ask, God answers. The moment was not a substitute because a substitute can never take the place of an original. This is an absolute and a treasured portion of the sacredness of loss. There will never be another to take the place of the one we have lost, but because Christ became our substitute and assumed sin's obligation, God's redeeming power retrieves the drowning heart and overcomes the lie that says death is the only conclusion. Christ will not make light of your loss by taking the place of the one you love, but the love that held Him on the cross amputates death's grip, obliterates sin's objections, and overshadows grief's audacity. The loving provision of Jesus Christ transcends the death of an anniversary with a birthday, bestows the grace of friendship amidst humanity's inability to get along, leads a lost soul home and restores what the locusts had eaten with a wedding feast, and provides a family portrait of the future with a snapshot from the past.

Dear Sister in Christ, when John said that Jesus is the propitiation for our sins (1 John 2:2), he did not only mean

He appeased the wrath of God toward our sin and made the way for us to be reconciled to Him. The gracious act of appeasement also means we now have access to the mercy seat of God, which is the saint's throne of grace and communion. The equivalent word in Hebrew for propitiation means "covering," as in the lid of the ark of the covenant, where the shed blood of sacrifice covers our sin and redeems our pain. This act of hallowed exchange literally means "to make favorable."[29] Jesus exchanged heaven's favor to make your life favorable—even in grief. Sin and death assaulted mankind, but Jesus assaulted them back. Evil tried to eclipse the Light, but the Light was the life of men, and His radiance could not be concealed.

Your husband is gone, but not his memory. Christ cancels our debt—not the person whose love we are indebted to. Your husband is not here, but what radiates from his life still emanates from behind your loss like the sun behind the moon's eclipse. My Friend, *My Friend*, grief will wane, but what was—what was sweet and good—is still yours. Even what you want to forget will bear fruit, and God will continue to give a bounty for what was loss and will satisfy your questions with His favor. He is not cruel or unjust and will not forget your love and what you have suffered, just as you do not forget His love and what He has suffered; only He'll do it better—a lot better. He's God, after all. His favor will continue to illuminate, to extend beyond your pain, to radiate warmth, and to outshine the darkness. His favor will be expressed in unexpected blessings, gifts, grace, and kindness, and it may all show up in the strangest of places and will always shine from behind the eclipse of your gloom.

For the vision is yet for the appointed time; it hastens toward the goal and it will not fail. Though it tarries, wait for it; for it will certainly come, it will not delay.

Habakkuk 2:3 NASB

It will also come to pass that before they call, I will answer; and while they are still speaking I will hear.

Isaiah 65:24 NASB

The lines have fallen to me in pleasant places; indeed, my heritage is beautiful to me.

Psalm 16:6 NASB

Even before a word is on my tongue, behold, O Lord, you know it altogether. You hem me in, behind and before, and lay your hand upon me.

Psalm 139:4–5 ESV

Twenty-Eight

Yearbooks

bob was gone. The afternoon's rain was turning its face away, moving east, and the deep purple and gray of evening's color had just arrived. I sat next to him in a sort of numb silence though it felt like I was screaming.

"Don't go," I said. "I can't live without you."

I don't know why I didn't say it before he died. I don't ever remember thinking about it until then. Rudy was sitting next to me on the floor, alert and quiet, sensing the moment as animals do, and Pastor Rich had arrived and was standing there in the stillness beside me. I wondered if Bob would have stayed if I had said the words while he was alive.

There are so many opinions about words and their value or appropriateness. Maybe if I had said those words while he was alive, it would have been *harder* for him to go, but really—it was already hard. It was impossible. Maybe if I had said the words it would have made it *easier* for him to go. Knowing one is loved is empowering. To die knowing you have done your job well and have sown love and received the fruit of that labor is a priceless legacy. To know you are deeply and desperately loved would be sublime. Knowing that the love you gave strengthened the ones left behind and enabled them to carry on would be a great reward.

The Word of God is the authority for all words. Jesus is the Word, and He confronts mankind with the possibilities and power of words available to him for his benefit or abuse. Death and life are in the power of the tongue. Words are never to corrupt but only to give grace, and they always indicate the condition of the heart. Our words can be swords of destruction, or they can be sweet and bring healing. We will give account of words spoken because out of the same mouth we bless God and curse man. Words can set the entire course of a life on fire or raise the dead to life. A word spoken at the right time is like golden apples set in silver, but wrongly employed, it can spew poison and be used to deceive.

There is a time to be silent and a time to speak; this is where the scale seeks its unattainable balance.

How can it be true that there is nothing more powerful in the whole world than a word, but at the same time it can also be true that a word not spoken can be the wisest word of all? Which is sadder, a word spoken that should have been kept or a word kept that should have been spoken? Do words mean more as time passes or less? Grief requires words, but words can never contain its entire meaning.

Each morning before Bob went to the fire station and before the sun was up, he knelt beside each of us individually, prayed, gave a kiss, and said he loved us. We usually slept through the expression of love, but the words were said.

The homeschool group we belonged to put together a lovely yearbook where the parents of seniors were invited to write words of wisdom, love, encouragement, and counsel to their student. Bob was full of life when Jennifer graduated and was able to pen on paper some of what his father-heart lived to express each day. When Samuel was a senior, Bob was more than halfway through his battle, but though already gaunt and atrophied, his hand held steady enough to articulate his heart once again.

Bob didn't live to see Benjamin graduate, but while he was still with us, the likelihood of death constrained me to swallow reality and ask him to use what strength he had to write to his youngest son. If he was not to survive, at least his words would. If the Lord healed him, the words would mean even more. Either way, Ben would have the legacy of his dad's words in his high school yearbook as did his sister and brother. I kept the original copy of the yearbook message in a safe until the time came for Ben to graduate and the sacred words would live on and fulfill their purpose.

Reality presented yet another opportunity for words to heal before death's blow. I understood regret to be a terrible enemy and made the decision to step in its way. I wanted to make sure the kids each had time to sit with their dad and tell him how much they loved him, what he meant to them, and anything else that was on their hearts. It was the most unbearable request I've ever made. Ironically, the two oldest don't remember much of what they said. They remember despising its necessity but understood the significance of the act and were deeply grateful to have had the chance. Ben was only eleven or twelve but clearly recalls the day he sat by his dad and told him he loved him, that he'd be okay, and that he would take care of me. And then, in the unfathomable grief of a boy needing the right words, Ben told his dad not to worry about the grass or the yard; he would take care of them.

Time has passed since those words found their rightful place in our lives. The color of grief continues to change with the backdrop of its seasons, but the importance of what we had the chance to say then now sheds light on what I didn't know. My Friend, I want you to listen: I thought that the words we expressed before Bob died would be enough. I thought we would look back and be satisfied. They were priceless words without exception, but the greater gift is that there are never enough words and there is never enough time to say all that love means, so there is freedom from the regret of not having enough time to say what we wanted. There are not enough words in this life to finish what needs to be said, and there are certain feelings that lose their meaning if put to words anyway.

Dear Friend, God did not mean for love's conversation to end just because one is no longer present. *We still have so much to say to him.* We still have so much to tell him because there's so much more life to tell him about. Life goes on and continues to fill our words with importance and urgency. There is so much life Bob is not a part of, and we are always saying, "I wish he was here," or "I wish he could meet his granddaughters," or "I wonder what Dad would say," or a thousand other "what ifs" and "if onlys." There never was enough time because time alone is not enough. God is not bound by time, but Satan tries to chain the boulder of regret to a grieving heart and throw it off a bridge to drown.

If you think you did not have enough time, I want you to know that I feel the same way as you; and we had time.

Dear Reader, it is the work of grief you must do, not the fruitless work of regret. You must cast off regret because death is always outside of your control, but the pain of what could have been can be repaired. It is your Christ who will tear up the invitation to regret's banquet for you. It is a sour feast and will cause you only illness; cast it off into His care. Honor the one you have lost in godly grief, not in regret, because godly sorrow leads to repentance and produces life. Regret condemns, but there is no condemnation for those who are in Christ Jesus. If you are carrying the burden of regret, the cure comes with its abandonment. Time is God's to control; do not let regret steal it from you any longer because regret . . . is the only thing there is never enough time for.

> *For the sorrow that is according to the will of God produces a repentance without regret, leading to salvation, but the sorrow of the world produces death.*
> 2 Corinthians 7:10 NASB

Twenty-Nine

The Ark

*You shall put into the ark the testimony which I shall
give you.*

Exodus 25:16 NASB

here are portions of what grief has served you that are too
bitter to digest. They sit in the bottom of your soul and
feel as though they will never be absorbed or broken down
into anything that can be assimilated for use.

I have memories that I will not write of here. Those
moments were the portions of grief that would not yield or
soften or heal. They always entered without knocking and made

themselves at home without invitation. I could not use them as seed to sow for the future because they would not grow, and even if they did burgeon into something that mimicked life, it would only be a foul counterfeit. The burden of the memories could not be thrown to the wind as chaff because they were too heavy with grief to be abandoned. The recollection of their pain was too personal to give away, but too unbearable to keep. I needed to do something with that pain because it was still a sacred piece of our testimony, but I could not carry it through my desert anymore. The intrusive images did not seem to belong in heaven or hell and ended up lodged somewhere in the corner of grief's purgatory.

The ark of the testimony carried the tablets of stone designated to bear the Ten Commandments of God. The ark was never carried anywhere in pomp or ceremonial procession but was packed and concealed from the eyes of the Israelites and the ones who bore its weight on their shoulders. When the tabernacle was pitched to house it, the ark was always kept in solemn darkness excluding any natural light, protecting the grandeur of its purpose. The only light to illumine the tabernacle shone day and night from the golden lamp as a constant reminder of God's presence and of Jesus, the Light of the World who was to come and always stay.

The elaborate style of the ark symbolized the great treasure it held. The stone tablets of God's commands were the direct testimony of Yahweh against sin in man and a venerable declaration that said no to death while reuniting humanity to God.[30] The ark was a moveable testimony displaying God's divine presence and was the evidence of His unalterable covenant. The words of the covenant were a kind of spiritual portrait of God and spoke of things to come on earth and in heaven—a time when Jesus would enter history by a new and living way that would fulfill the law's purpose and inaugurate the transfer of the burden of sin to His shoulders. The new covenant was from then on to be carried by Jesus alone.

Believer, the measure of your grief's testimony that is too personal to give away, but too unbearable to keep can be safely enveloped in the divine presence of Jesus; place it in the ark of His care. The trauma of its most vile wounds must stay in the solemn darkness where His presence promises to watch over it but protect you from its further harm. The calamity and violation of your loss is sacred because it is connected to the one you have loved, but some portions are unfathomable to a human heart. They burrow a hole in your gut and stay, uninvited and void of purpose except to trespass, assault, and profane. Their words are like tar, and their taunts bludgeon and lie. These memories will push you on the floor, put their foot on your back, and tell you to stay there where you will always be their prisoner and victim; but it does not have to be so.

Place the memories in the ark of His care. He understands their sacredness and role in your testimony, but the memories are not your loved one and are not to be your ruler or idol. You do not have to look at them any longer, but you must do something with them. They are a dark piece of your testimony, but the depth of pain somehow explains the value. The weight is not to be your burden any longer if you will dare to hand it over into God's safekeeping and exchange it for the easier burden that Christ offers. You must relinquish its control, or it will control you and strangle the progress and hope of healthy grief.

In handing over this portion, you are declaring your protest against sin and death. This is your real testimony. This is the evidence that you have loved and verifies the merit of what you have suffered. The darkest times will not control your future but instead be put in their place—in the ark of His care—and remain as the holy contents of what are now your credentials and magnum opus.

There is no need for pomp or procession; your grief is far too precious and is above the worth of such a display. Place your darkest pain in His care. This quiet transfer of responsibility will be a constant reminder of His presence and covenant and will remain a joint declaration against death between you and your God. Your testimony will be true because it will tell the story of God's faithfulness and infallibility. Your testimony will be able to move forward in its beautiful purpose as a testimony should. And, Dear Saint, you will be able to bear it.

The law of the Lord is perfect, restoring the soul; the testimony of the Lord is sure, making wise the simple.
Psalm 19:7 NASB

And they have conquered him by the blood of the Lamb and by the word of their testimony, for they loved not their lives even unto death.
Revelation 12:11 ESV

Come and hear, all you who fear God, and I will tell what He has done for my soul.

Psalm 66:16 ESV

For this reason I also suffer these things, but I am not ashamed; for I know whom I have believed and I am convinced that He is able to guard what I have entrusted to Him until that day.

2 Timothy 1:12 NASB

Thirty

Rest

Come to Me, all you who labor and are heavy-laden, and I will give you rest. Take My yoke upon you and learn from Me, for I am gentle and lowly in heart, and you will find rest for your souls.

Matthew 11:28 NKJV

T his quiet scripture in Matthew 11 invites you to *come*. Jesus was focused on you when He said it, and His gentleness bids you to draw near in your exhaustion. He asks that you come absolutely, exclusively, and continuously to Him in whose presence there is rest.

Labor in this scripture's context is defined as the most wearisome type in which the worker gives all they have, without a break and without end. It is an internal weariness that feels as though one has been beaten to the point of losing heart and giving up.[31]

Your *heavy laden-ness* is, in a way, the assurance that you have packed appropriately for the journey. The expression is derived from a military term and describes the expected load every soldier was required to carry. The weight of the backpack was determined by the length of the journey and carried with it the connotation of a person who had much of it still ahead.[32]

The promised *rest* of God is the believer's desperately needed opportunity to stop and catch their breath on the steep climb of their toil. To rest is to breathe, not to *hold one's breath.* In Christ, rest is accompanied by refreshment and the relaxing of strained emotional muscles. Jesus offers a Sabbath rest in the midst of a soul's labor.

To *take* the yoke Jesus offers seems like a painful paradox, but here God is not asking an already bent-over believer to take on a yoke of servitude and oppression. There is no added weight with the yoke of Christ, but only a lifting of it. His yoke is His promise of unbreakable fellowship and unity. Simply taking His yoke and putting it on changes the atmosphere of life. The word *yoke* comes from a root word meaning "to join" or "unite" and is representative of a bond between two people who become joined to work together as one—a marriage of sorts.

A wedding ring represents the bond between two people who become joined as one, making an unending pledge to mutually and willingly take on the burden of marital love that would be too heavy for one person to carry alone. Many myths have surrounded the significance of wearing the ring on the fourth finger. Some say it is placed there because when a priest prayed over a marriage, he would do so in the name of the Father, Son, and Holy Spirit, touching each finger and saying "amen" at the fourth—"amen" sealing the marriage. Other romantics have imagined there is a vein in the fourth finger connecting to the heart. Some believe the ring started out on the pinky because it is the least-used finger, but it was then moved to the fourth finger because a ring small enough to fit on a pinky did not allow enough room for jewels or decoration.

A wedding ring is not heavy in weight, but heavy in meaning, like the yoke Jesus offers to the weary and broken soul. A ring is a public statement, an outward symbol of inward commitment, and a wedding ring always tells a story. A wedding ring is not only a reminder of the vows two individuals give and receive, one to the other, but it is also a symbol of God's eternal faithfulness toward His children, promising to keep their marriage united in a way that would not be possible on their own.

Because the effects of Bob's illness began on his left side, the ring finger of his left hand quickly atrophied and was unable to hold his wedding ring. We put it away in a drawer for safekeeping and with hope. After he died, I placed the ring on a gold chain and wore it around my neck. It was light in weight, but heavy in meaning. The ring was still an outward symbol of inward commitment, and it told a story. The gold band would always be a symbol of God's eternal faithfulness and was a reminder that He had kept our marriage united through life and death in a way that we could not have done on our own. But I knew our rings could not be worn into eternity because the earthly must one day be exchanged for the heavenly at another wedding.

To *learn* from Jesus means accepting what He says as true, so much so that we intentionally apply what we learn until His ways emerge as our lifelong habits. In ancient times, students learned from a particular rabbi by attaching themselves to that rabbi, serving and living at his side and trusting him as their absolute authority until they transformed to reflect their teacher in every way. In return, the rabbi provided shelter, food, and protection.[33] We resolve to attach ourselves to Him just as a student attaches himself to his rabbi, serving and living by His side and trusting Him as our absolute authority until our transformation reflects our teacher.

Christ's *gentleness* is not to be misunderstood as weakness. On the contrary, true gentleness is strength under control—limitless power under love's mighty restraint. He is lowly in heart because even as God, He is inscrutably dependent on His Father. He exchanged the yoke of royalty for commonplace obscurity, and it is there in His kingly approachability that you will find your rest and be able to breathe. What you discover as you take His easy yoke will be your *eureka*, the Greek word for *find*. You will finally find what you have been looking for.

My Friend, we have rounded the bend and have been leaning hard on God, depending on Him for our very breath. How gracious He has been. But the journey's destination is still ahead. Your Christ often gathered His disciples into the embrace of the wilderness to rest and be restored. Believer, do not mistake your season here as a barren wasteland of nothing more than added burdens of a merciless God. He has brought you here to the only oasis in the desert. He does not require you to take on a yoke of heaviness, but to transfer the weight of your burden and allow Him to carry the load. Accept what He says as true. Come and bow with relief under the burdenless weight of His yoke. It is tailor-made and lined with His rest. Under its ease, you will find what you have been looking for.

The wedding ring symbolized the bond of unity between you and your husband, but it was meant to be shouldered by two. The weight of it has grown heavy now without him, but if you will hand its burden over to your God in exchange for His yoke of provision, you will find that it becomes light in weight once again. Unpack and rest. Stay and learn and breathe. In the name of the Father, the Son, and the Holy Spirit, amen.

After a year or so, I took the ring from around my neck and placed it in a special box with other sacred tokens of a loving marriage. The burden of it is lighter now, but still weighty in meaning. As a matter of fact, the meaning continues to grow and burgeon with time. I slowly gave up its burden without giving up its meaning. It was a good exchange.

So there remains a Sabbath rest for the people of God. For the one who has entered His rest has himself also rested from his works, as God did from His.
Hebrews 4:10 NASB

For I have satiated the weary soul, and every grieved soul I have filled.
Jeremiah 31:25 YLT

Thirty-One

Sanctus

n the absence of the original head of her family, a widow's authority is divided and multiplied all at the same time. Though she was a coauthority inside the family unit before her husband died, the mysterious tearing that has divided what was once one, unceremoniously leaves everything to her care alone. It is God's original plan for a wife to be sheltered under her husband's haven of support, where she is safe and free to live and flow in God's gifts and ministry. To submit is, ideally, to be strengthened and raised up to a rightful position within God's calling. A wife's position is so sacred that the world is often offended and hostile toward such a beautiful expression of noble humility, and the enemy of God and mankind works to cause its demise and exploitation; but all is not lost, Dear Believer.

Our English word *authority* comes from a Latin word meaning "to create, increase, augment or nourish."[34] The authority that was yours in marriage is now newly created, increased, augmented, and to be nourished by the only one from whom authority is given. Romans 13:1 from the Amplified Version explains your position: "For there is no authority except from God [by His permission, His sanction]." His authority sanctions your equipping for the task ahead because the word *sanction* comes from *sanctus*, which means "holy," confirming that what God sanctions is an inviolable decree.[35] He calls into existence that which has not yet been, and He will make all things new for you. His umbrella of authority is your sanctuary, your *sanctus*, a holy place of refuge and sustenance, and it is from here you will be able to extend sanctuary to others. He who calls you is faithful.

In a dream, I had made room for an unwelcome visitor. He challenged my authority in my home, but without fanfare. I had hardly even noticed. The stranger must have been waiting quietly until I was numb to his presence because in my dream, he simply walked into our living room one morning and sat down. He was covered with dirt and old blankets and looked quite homeless, but he never showed his face. In turning to look at him, I noticed the whole house was suddenly covered in a film of dirt, but before I could make an accusation, he threw one of his blankets over my head and somehow, without a word, removed my presence from the room. I could still see the kids, but the life newly given to me to oversee alone was being overthrown in some sort of spiritual coup d'etat. The ones who were supposed to be safe under my wing of authority were no longer aware of my presence. The intruder did not remove me from our home; he just made me irrelevant.

God's counsel and warning were kind, and His exhortation came before any damage had been done, but I needed to understand that God ordained my position of authority. If I was to protect my children, resources, and future, and do so without my husband, I could succeed only by trusting God's promise. He would be faithful to increase, nourish, and augment. What troubled me was the deep weariness of widowed existence. Taking on what looked like doubled responsibility crushed the layers of grief that were already bruised and tender to the touch; but it was not my ability I needed to have confidence in—it was His. It was not my ability that defined my authority—it was His. I did not have to step up—I was already there. God was not only my authority, sanction, sanctuary, father, and bridegroom, *but now He was my husband as well.*

Under His sanctuary there is no end to His abundance because "He who supplies seed to the sower and bread for food will supply and multiply your seed for sowing and increase the harvest of your righteousness" (2 Corinthians 9:10 ESV). He has given permission and freedom to you and me to exercise His authority. All that is required of us is to stay within His embrace and consent. It is called abiding, and apart from Him, it is impossible to do because only in Him, and only under His sanctuary, can we really live, move, and flourish. He who began the good work of your faith will finish it. Your title has changed; His promise has not.

Therefore, do not throw away your confidence which has a great reward.
Hebrews 10:35 NASB

So take a new grip with your tired hands and stand firm on your shaky legs. Mark out a straight path for your feet. Then those who follow you, though they are weak and lame, will not stumble and fall but will become strong.
Hebrews 12:12–13 NLT

God, who calls you, is faithful; he will do this.
1 Thessalonians 5:24 NLT

If iniquity is in your hand—put it far away, and do not let evil reside in your tents.
Job 11:14 NET

If you do well, will not your countenance be lifted up? And if you do not do well, sin is crouching at the door; and its desire is for you, but you must master it.
Genesis 4:7 NASB

He will bless them that fear the Lord, both small and great. The Lord shall increase you more and more, you and your children.
Psalm 115:13–14 KJV

You have made a wide path for my feet to keep them from slipping.

Psalm 18:36 NLT

Greatness, power, splendor, glory, and majesty are yours, Lord, because everything in heaven and on earth is yours. The kingdom is yours, Lord, and you are honored as head of all things. Riches and honor are in front of you. You rule everything. You hold power and strength in your hands, and you can make anyone great and strong.

1 Chronicles 29:11–12 GW

Thirty-Two

Dry Bones

Our bones are dried up, our hope is lost; we are indeed cut off.

Ezekiel 37:11 ESV

I n chapter 37 of Ezekiel, the prophet was transported to a vision that renewed the hope of Israel. Like you, Dear Friend, the Lord set Ezekiel down in the middle of a valley where He breathed life into dry bones and promised to restore what had been destroyed. Israel's fate was dismal, but the prophet's words say otherwise and are followed by the breath of God that you and I have become so familiar with on our journey. For a widow, more than anyone else, with the promise of restoration comes a piercing invitation: when it is time, will you accept whatever future calling God has for you and obey your trustworthy Christ, no matter how weak and desperate you feel right now? I ask the question because it is only out of that weakness and desperation that He desires to identify you as His example of perseverance and prayer against the world's corruption and assault in the last days.

Faithful Friend, God empowers the believer with the gift of choice and opportunity, but a decision must be made whether to accept or decline. As you face your calling, you will need to make that decision within the steadfast hope of what you do not see yet and with the understanding that though your bones feel dried up, they are not buried, and though your hope seems lost, it has never been missing. Yes, to be a widow is a set-apart calling, but in the midst of it, you will never, ever, be cut off from your Shepherd.

The truth of what is ahead for you must be found in God's Word. You will see there that you are meant to be one of His greatest allies in these times of faint hearts and tribulation. As a widow, you have been called for a great and unique purpose. Because of what you have suffered, you know that His grace is sufficient and His power is perfected and strong in your weakness and limitations. The power of Christ rests on you, dwells in you, and steadies you. He is your hope, and He will not disappoint you.

The Hebrew word for hope is *tiqvah* and when translated means "absolute assurance of future good." The believer's hope is never "hope so" but always "hope sure."[36] My Widowed

Friend, we do not grieve without hope, and our future will not be won without hope either. Faith is the assurance of things hoped for, and in the future, when you have to fight for something (and you will), you must arm yourself with the assurance of that hope because . . . your God has a plan for you. A plan so important His Word identifies a widow's lowly position as a beacon of instruction for the body of Christ. Out of all the possible examples Jesus could have used to illustrate how believers must press through the tribulation of these end times, He chose a widow. Against all odds and with unabashed godly tenacity, the widow in Luke 18 is linked to Luke 17 and the final crisis of the last days:

> *Then* [after all he had just spoken to them about the devastation to come] *Jesus told His disciples a parable to teach them that they should always pray and never become discouraged. In a certain town there was a judge who neither feared God nor respected people. And there was a widow in that same town who kept coming to him and pleading for her rights, saying, "Help me against my opponent!" For a long time the judge refused to act, but at last he said to himself, "Even though I don't fear God or respect people, yet because of all the trouble this widow is giving me, I will see to it that she gets her rights. If I don't, she will keep on coming and finally wear me out." And the Lord continued, "Listen to what that corrupt judge said. Now will God not judge in favor of His own people who cry to Him day and night for help? Will He be slow to help them? I tell you, He*

will judge in their favor and do it quickly. But will the
Son of Man find faith on earth when He comes?"
Luke 18:1-8 GNT

In the parable of the persistent widow, Jesus admonished all believers to pray at all times and not lose heart, and then He put a widow center stage. In those particular times, judges held court in tents and were often known to have their own agendas that could be swayed by a little compensation. In other words, if someone wanted to have their case heard, they would have to buy off the judge. He was generally an unrighteous, callous, and self-centered man, but the widow's glory was in her lowly position. Being isolated and having her status in the world regularly assaulted was a way of life for her, but Scripture says the judge, in all the weight and status of his position, was no match for her. In Greek, the phrase "she kept coming" is a boxing term for hitting someone in the eye repeatedly. She was at the end of her rope but knew the system and how things worked, and she knew God's strength prevailed in weakness. And she was victorious.

Dear Treasured Saint, if your victory is assured in the unjust courts of this life, how much more are your future conquests secured under the protective abundance of the throne of grace? You are God's own, and He is your defense; He hears your wounded cry, and He protects you. He breathes life into your dry bones so that you may stand upright in your new calling to exhort the rest of the body of Christ to always pray and not lose heart.

When the Son of Man comes, will He find faith on the earth? I believe He will. He will find a widow's faith. He will find yours.

So I prophesied as He commanded me, and the breath came into them, and they came to life and stood on their feet, an exceedingly great army.
Ezekiel 37:10 NASB

Therefore, do not throw away your confidence, which has a great reward. For you have need of endurance, so that when you have done the will of God, you may receive what was promised.
Hebrews 10:35–16 NASB

Therefore let us draw near with confidence to the throne of grace, so that we may receive mercy and find grace to help in time of need.
Hebrews 4:16 NASB

Therefore, my beloved brethren, be steadfast, immovable, always abounding in the work of the Lord, knowing that your toil is not in vain in the Lord.
1 Corinthians 15:58 NASB

Rejoicing in hope, persevering in tribulation, devoted to prayer.
Romans 12:12 NASB

For the foolishness of God is wiser than men, and the weakness of God is stronger than men. For consider your calling, brethren: not many of you were wise according to worldly standards, not many were powerful, not many of noble birth. But God chose what is foolish in the world to shame the wise; God chose what is weak in the world to shame the strong; God chose what is low and despised in the world, even things that are not, to bring to nothing things that are, so that no human being might boast in the presence of God. And because of him you are in Christ Jesus, who became to us wisdom from God, righteousness and sanctification and redemption so that, as it is written, "Let the one who boasts, boast in the Lord."

1 Corinthians 1:25–31 ESV

"My grace is sufficient for you, for My power is made perfect in weakness." Therefore I will boast all the more gladly of my weaknesses, so that the power of Christ may rest upon me. For the sake of Christ, then, I am content with weaknesses, insults, hardships, persecutions, and calamities. For when I am weak, then I am strong.

2 Corinthians 12:9–10 ESV

Thirty-Three

Settling

How firm a foundation, ye saints of the Lord, is laid for your faith in His excellent Word! What more can He say than to you He hath said, to you who for refuge to Jesus have fled?

John Keith (1787), "How Firm a Foundation"

a fire truck always commands respect and attention, but that day there were no lights or sirens to be seen or heard from the big rig. That day, sitting atop Engine 93, was a casket, and it held our world inside. The casket's sacred contents were carried in agonizing reverence off the truck and then to the graveside by Bob's brothers, our son Samuel, and our friend Roland. There couldn't have been a more royal ceremony—so many family members and friends, "Amazing Grace" and bagpipes, and the toll of the final bell.

The barrenness of death was settling in on us all and making itself at home, but not enough to convince me yet that he was really gone. How is one to accept the fact that a whole lifetime could simply be lowered into the ground where the sacred would be made common and covered with dirt?

We left before the last humiliation of an honorable life took place and the ground was irreverently pushed and pressed to settle around one of God's treasures. The next day I went back to Bob's grave, as I did every day for many months. With each visit, the small mound of dirt covering his grave settled slowly into the earth. Grief was doing the same and settled slowly into our unsettled world.

Roland and his family are our dearest friends. A friendship takes time to cultivate and build, and the soil under its foundation must be solid enough to withstand the elements of life. Their friendship has stood that test, and there is none better. We had been friends for over twenty years when Bob died, and it was appropriate that Roland come alongside his friend Bob one more time and carry his body safely to rest.

Roland is a contractor. He built our house. He's one of those guys who can see the finished project before the building has begun. He started building our home in the middle of winter and had to pay special attention to the condition of the soil before setting the foundation in place. Left on its own, the ground can take years to settle. To support a structure, the soil must be settled, or the foundation will fail and the home will be compromised. If solid ground is disturbed, great care must be taken to compact it again before building, so a lot depends on the magnitude of the disturbance and the severity of the weather patterns in the surrounding area. The greater the shifting of the soil, the greater the time needed to level it and make it suitable for building, and the more severe the weather conditions, the more care must be taken before construction can begin. The colder the temperature and steeper the slope, the deeper the digging has to be to ensure the elements won't cause the structure to fall. The process is calculated, planned, and very intentional.

The settling of grief under the foundation of your life has begun, and there is so much to consider. The disturbance underneath you has been great and requires time to settle; let it settle, Believer, because the future stability of what you build depends on how well the ground around your life has come to rest, and rushing through it will be detrimental. Take care not to bury the debris of your grief below the surface; it will degrade over time and your house will shift and crack. God will sift it for you if you will be patient, and then only the good soil will remain. Let grief settle and you will not sink under its weight. He will press the earth firmly around your roots and you will stand, but give it time.

In his kindness God called you to share in his eternal glory by means of Christ Jesus. So after you have suffered a little while, he will restore, support and strengthen you, and he will place you on a firm foundation.

1 Peter 5:10 NLT

Thirty-Four

Faithful

There is nothing that can replace the absence of someone dear to us, and one should not even attempt to do so. One must simply hold out and endure it. At first that sounds very hard, but at the same time it is also a great comfort. For to the extent the emptiness truly remains unfilled one remains connected to the other person through it. It is wrong to say that God fills the emptiness. God in no way fills it but much more leaves it precisely unfilled and thus helps us preserve—even in pain—the authentic relationship. Furthermore, the more beautiful the remembrances, the more difficult the separation. But gratitude transforms the torment of memory into silent joy. One bears what was lovely in the past not as a thorn but as a precious gift deep within, a hidden treasure of which one can always be certain.

Dietrich Bonhoeffer

Parts of grief always seem to keep showing up. They don't ever get *filled up* or *used up*; they just *show up* and continue their journey and ministry.

My dad died on Christmas Eve 1995 while my brother and I held his hand and with his wonderful wife beside him. So many years have passed, but I still catch myself thinking that I need to call him and tell him this or that. Grief continues and can become a comforting treasure. Grief should move, but one never simply "moves on."

My friend Robbie asked me once, "Did you know that God stares at you?" He said it when I was feeling quite alone and needed encouragement. I needed to be reminded one more time that God's eyes are ever on His beloved, but I had never heard it said in such a dramatically personal way. Robbie died tragically and much too soon, but I still remember his simple, profound words and often find myself telling others what he said. Grief continues to teach, and its lessons never end.

My brother Steve and I share the mysterious connection that cements the unique, often strange and indestructible love between siblings. The night our mom took her life, he was already there at her apartment talking to the police when I arrived and without words wrapped his arm around my horror and steadied my pain with his. The police needed someone to identify her body, and Steve stepped up without hesitating to do the unthinkable. On the day of our dad's funeral, he folded his arm around me again, and we walked together one more time toward another grave.

Minutes before Bob died, Steve showed up at our house. We didn't know he was coming, and neither did he. That morning he just knew he had to come. After the kids and I saw Bob off, I went out into the living room, and a brother's arms met me there again. These were the worst moments of life, and they are among the greatest moments of life too. The separation of death results in grief, but grief unites too.

The occupation of firefighting carries with it a certain dignity, but that day, one of the city's finest sat on my front porch after driving around trying to deal with Bob's death. He was drunk and crying and not very dignified. It was springtime and the sun was kind, so we sat and talked for a while outside, and when he was collected and had recovered his balance and dignity, I watched him slowly drive down the canyon. He came back one more time during the next year, and we sat and mended on the front porch under the sunshine again. Grief steals our dignity sometimes. Accepting grief gives it back.

Nine years have passed since Bob died. Reminiscing about his life and death doesn't derail us as much anymore, but it can still give us a good shove, and that it should. For the most part, these days we decide if and when a heart-to-heart with the past should be convened, but we have also learned to count on the irregular regularity of grief's impromptu visits.

Last December it showed up in Ben's car. He used to drive my old Saturn Vue, but when Jennifer and Lee were expecting their first baby, we all thought it made more sense for them to have a four-door and Ben could have Jenn's two-door Honda, so they made the trade. Their dad was a fireman, and cars were routinely cleaned out, but God's timing is inscrutable. Somehow a small piece of paper had, for the last eight years, remained hidden in a car that had been cleaned out and scrubbed a hundred times. Ben found it one day while he was cleaning the Honda. It was a letter to Jennifer from Bob. The words were penned in the love of a dad to his girl and included a scripture. Ben decided to frame the letter and give it to his sister for Christmas. The timing was perfect and the gift overwhelming in its significance. The scripture was the same one Jenn and Lee had previously adopted as their go-to verse in times of hardship and discouragement. Bob had died five years before Lee and Jennifer ever met.

The mysterious friendship of grief continues to move and perplex us all. It can show up on Christmas Eve, in the simple words of a lost friend, on the front porch, or on the floor of a car. Oddly enough, grief has become a bit of a faithful friend, and we look forward to its kindness showing up in the most unexpected places and in the most wondrous of ways.

It might take some time, but when you can, if you look, you will see it too.

Faithful are the wounds of a friend.
Proverbs 27:6 KJV

Thirty-Five

Firsts and Lasts

I am the Alpha and the Omega, the first and the last, the
beginning and the end.
Revelation 22:13 NASB

b ob sat across from his mom and dad and told them in
Spanish he was dying. The appropriate words for such
a time have never been created, so they didn't say very
much. Each minute that followed was the first and last of its
kind, and the air felt dry and coarse, almost as if it were an old
forest overgrown with pins and needles. I can feel the memory
catch and pull on my skin even now as I walk through its image.

The conversation was nearly wordless, and it was the beginning of their good-bye.

Three years later his beautiful mom and dad and youngest brother Jimmy sat by his bed the day before he died. The appropriate words for such a time have never been created, so they didn't say very much. The air was coarse and stagnant, and the conversation was nearly wordless once again. I knew it was the last time they would see Bob and that the nearly wordless conversation was the beginning of a lifelong good-bye.

Firsts and lasts, beginnings and endings seem to signify the most meaningful poignancies of human existence. "Firsts" come before all others; they are the "foremosts" of life and mark things not previously done or experienced. To be first describes the character of an original in preference or position: "the first of its kind" or "first in his field." The first is the highest of all parts of anything and is before anything else.[37]

"Lasts" come after all others in time, order, or place. The last moment comes before the next moment or before moving on and is always the only one remaining of its kind. It is final; it is the ultimate and the conclusion. In reference to prestige or importance, the last comes after all others in suitability or likelihood. The last is the least desirable and exemplifies the utmost and extreme of all things despised. The last always takes longer. When someone "breathes their last," it is always the most painful, but "to last" can mean to continue on and finish the course.[38] If someone or something lasts, they or it remain and continue . . . like a memory.

The beginning is the point of time or space at which anything commences. The beginning is the origin, source, or opening and it must happen before proceeding and in order to perform the earliest part of whatever comes next. To begin is to open.[39]

The end is the last part and is a point, line, or limitation that indicates the full extent or degree of something. The end is the limit or bounds, the furthermost imaginable place. The end is the intention or aim and is the object for which a thing exists—its purpose. The "end all" of something can constitute the most outstanding or greatest possible example or instance. To end means to reach or arrive at a final condition or goal. If you are at your wits' end, you are at the end of your ideas or mental resources.[40]

Immediately after every first has transpired, it becomes the last of its kind and makes way for the next first.

If we were to continue meandering around this circle of reason, we would in fact arrive at our wits' end because the thought process would eventually consume itself and us with it. The truth that Jesus Christ is the Alpha and Omega, the beginning and the end, is the Infinite's explanation of what the finite cannot comprehend: Jesus, the Father, and the Holy Spirit have always been or, to put it another way, have never not existed. They are outside of being. They do not end because they did not begin. They are beyond any concept of first or last and so far exceed description that even their names defy translation.

The Greek words *alpha* and *omega* translate into Hebrew as *aleph* and *tav*, the first and last letters of the Hebrew alphabet. But their divine meaning is far more than simply the first and last letters of the alphabet.

The two letters *aleph tav* appear together, on their own, in the Hebrew Scriptures over seven thousand times. Scholars have been unable to determine their meaning, and many deduce that they were intended to shift our gaze to the God who encompasses and exceeds all of human understanding—and invites us to stand in awe. *Aleph tav*'s definition remains inapprehensible by mankind, not because of a language deficit, but because there is no language to contain it. The untranslatable defines the indefinable and chooses to make the divine presence known where there are no words to contain its depth of meaning.

The great I AM fills all space and with His presence makes the empty chasm of grief burgeon with the unbreakable covenant presence of our *Aleph Tav*, the Alpha and Omega. He is where no appropriate words exist and where none would suffice anyway. Dear Friend, in what feels like a bottomless void spanning the unseen distance between you and your husband lives the Alpha and Omega, the *Aleph Tav*, the untranslatable. The very rift that separates you is what connects you because Jesus is everywhere, including beyond and outside of everywhere. He understands your indefinable pain because He is indefinable and inhabits the inexpressible.

Here in this empty place lives the fullness of the triune God. He is the highest of all the unreachable parts of your grief, and He is before and after the rest of your grief. Your Alpha and Omega was in the last moment of your husband's death, and He is your next moment of life. Jesus Christ became the last and lowest in prestige and importance and humbled Himself so His presence could join you to heaven while you're still on earth. The emptiness that has stopped your life and feels like a brick wall is where He abides, but He cannot be stopped. He goes on; He continues; He will be your force, and He will last. He remains and will see to it that you survive the course.

Jesus is here in this point of time where your next breath begins and ends and begins again, and He will open the way before you because He *is* the Way. He is the full extent of what you need and is beyond your imagination. He is the one for whom you exist, your purpose and goal. He is the greatest possible outcome. When you are at the end of yourself, He is the great I AM. When you can't even begin to think of beginning again, He IS. Your Savior is your everything considered, your above all else, your altogether. Believer, He makes ends meet and begin again.

Thirty Six

Flags and Banners

Banners are made for the breeze, the sun, the battle.
Charles H. Spurgeon, *The Treasury of David*

Three flags remain, each folded in a triangle and encased in honor and love. One was flown at half-staff in front of Bob's last fire station the day he died and then presented to us by the chief at his funeral. The next two were given at state and national firefighter memorials. They do not fly anymore except in our hearts, but sit quietly in the homes of each of the kids, signifying the life of the man under whose name they were loved.

A flag or banner signifies the presence of a sovereign or indicates the call-to-arms of an army or fleet.[41] A banner can be held up as an expression of honor or love. Its appearance can indicate representation, herald an event, or even inspire unity. Some wear the banner of their love or country after a victory, and some bury their face or wipe their tears in it.

In the Bible, a banner demonstrates God's presence and can stand as a rallying point of healing for a person or a nation. God's banner puts the enemy to flight and marks a safe path for His people. A banner is a conspicuous proclamation and celebration. Banners signify hope, duty, and comfort and are often flown that a righteous cause might be vindicated and that God would be magnified.[42] Under God's banner of love, Christians gather and prepare, are inspired, directed, and carry the name of Christ to victory over sin, satan, and the world.

Kind Believer, you have come to this trysting place under the banner of Christ for many days now, and though its streamers do not catch in the wind right now, the emblem of your God still stands over you. You may yet dry your sorrows in its folds for a very long time, but the banner will stand. You and your family will rally again, and your path will be straight. Your proclamation will inspire, signify hope, call others to duty, and comfort the storm-tossed. Your banner will unfurl again, celebrating and signifying the God under whose name you are loved. Rest. There is no hurry.

Moses built an altar and named it, "The Lord is My Banner."

Exodus 17:15 NASB

We will sing for joy over your victory, and in the name of our God we will set up our banners. May the Lord fulfill all your petitions.

Psalm 20:5 NASB

You have given a banner to those who fear You, that it may be displayed because of the truth. Selah.

Psalm 60:4 NASB

ThirtySeven

Grief's Ovation

Who for the joy set before Him endured the cross, despising the shame, and has sat down at the right hand of the throne of God.

Hebrews 12:2 NASB

Jesus suffered as God and man without yielding to shame. It is unthinkable and unutterable. The gift of His suffering is unparalleled.

Charles Spurgeon said, "Upon any ordinary subject one may find liberty of speech and fullness of utterance, but this subject lies out of all oratory, and eloquence cannot attain unto it. None of us know the half of the agony which He endured; none of us have ever fully comprehended the love of Christ which passeth knowledge. Philosophers have probed the earth to its very center, threaded the spheres, measured the skies, weighed the hills—nay, weighed the world itself; but this is one of those vast, boundless things, which to measure doth surpass all but the Infinite itself."[43]

To suffer shame means to bow under the most contemptible humiliation of all. Shame lowers the most noble to outcast and beggar. Our matchless Christ suffered matchless humiliation because of His unequaled royalty. The Highest stooped the lowest and was numbered with the dregs of mankind, hung up naked with nails through His tender skin, mocked, mimicked, friendless, and covered with sinners' spit. He was charged with blasphemy, sedition, and treason. The King was made to wear the cloak of toy soldiers and shoved around by a pack of grade-school bullies, but He didn't stop them. He didn't stop them because He could not be stopped. There was something else in sight that consumed His passion so completely as to make shame look like a virtue in comparison.

Beloved, *you* were the joy set before Him. The shame meant so little compared to you. Jesus Christ sacrificed the ovation that was His royal due so you could partake of honor instead of shame. He sacrificed what should have been His renown and shifted eternity's spotlight onto the joy that constrained Him to endure the cross: you and me.

Creation is imprinted with God's character and beauty and originally knew no shame. Our word *shame* comes from a German word meaning "to cover." Before the fall of man's innocence, Adam and Eve were not ashamed—of anything. Afterwards, they felt the first malignant consequence of sin: the instinct to cover what was not meant to be hidden prior to sin's humiliating display.

Traditionally, firefighters celebrate their retirement with a dinner and festivities attended by their comrades, family, friends, and representatives from the department's upper echelons. Firefighting is a noble profession and carries with it a masculine dignity that is specific to its call. Bob personified that call and served among its noble ranks in the name of his Christ, but he also felt the shame of his mortality. Most of his fellow firefighters had not seen him in the few years following his diagnosis, and because Bob's body and ability to speak were so marred by the disease, he did not want them to see him.

Shame runs so deep and sings its dirge without mercy or respect, but the love of an honorable man for his God and gospel caused him to despise shame and endure his cross. And so, the evening came when Bob stood in front of the podium as a breath and shadow of who he had been and with a speech in his hands. He spoke slowly and deliberately so he could be understood and, I suppose, to give the angels and the great cloud of witnesses a chance to take their seats. His words were slurred and weak, but for that eleventh hour, shame had lost its grip.

"I didn't . . . want you . . . to see me . . . like this," he said.

Then, after a few introductory remarks, in the grandest act of humility I had ever witnessed, the man who was dying, the man whom everyone had come there to see and love and honor, shifted the spotlight. Bob began to talk about me. He said words that were too lovely to write here, and he asked for the honor of the moment to be given to his wife. The crowd rose and gave me a standing ovation.

The rest of the evening's story is still living, but in my memory it is a breath and shadow of what it was then. I know Bob talked about the kids and presented the gospel. I know we all hugged and kissed and cried. There was some laughter too, and food and presentations, but above all, I was changed because the man to whom honor was due gave it to me instead. I didn't earn it, and I knew I didn't deserve it. I honestly didn't know what he was talking about. He was the one who was dying. He was the one who stood despite his shame.

I think now, though, I might understand. Bob saw me at my worst and most humiliated too. He heard me cry during the night. He knew intimately what I went through, and he watched me experience what I cannot describe. He felt my pain and was all too aware of the burden that would be mine when he died. He knew what no one else would ever know about my suffering and saw what no one else would ever see, and he gave me an ovation for it.

I wanted to write this chapter for you, Dear Friend, because you weep without your husband now. You deserve an ovation for persevering even though you don't think you do or care right now or think anyone has noticed. I want to give you an ovation because Jesus died so that you could experience joy instead of shame. You should know that even if your husband did not die in Christ or with honor, your Savior has seen all that you have endured, and He thinks you're extraordinary. So do I. Jesus knows what no one else knows about your pain, and He sees what no one else sees. God your Father is pleased with you and grieves with you, and He and I are standing right now in your honor.

I want you to know, after I type these words, that I will applaud you with an ovation of tears and admiration. A great proclamation will ascend and declare your worth and future, and I give you my word that I will pray for you from this day forward until we meet Him in the air. I will not forget you and all that you have gone through. Because your righteousness has been experienced in the secret places of grief, God will reward you openly with joy. Hear His proclamation:

Your Father who sees what is done in secret will reward you.

Matthew 6:4 NASB

Thirty-Eight

Dross

What thou lov'st well remains,
The rest is dross.
What thou lov'st well shall not
Be reft from thee.
What thou lov'st well is thy true heritage.

Ezra Pound, The Pisan Cantos, No. 81

The kids grew up being loved and loving "very well." It is definitely their "true heritage." For Ben, his love was still young when his dad died, and as life has grown bigger, so has his grief. He mourned as deeply as any thirteen-year-old ever has, but grief requires tender and consistent care with each stage of life, and when Ben became a young man, each new loss, no matter its size, reopened the old. Such is the loyalty of grief.

Though Ben didn't get as many years with his dad as Jennifer and Samuel had, God's kindness (in hindsight) was expressed to him in a more subtle gift, because by the time Ben came along, Bob had gotten pretty comfortable with being the dad of a fragile, crying baby. He changed more diapers, cleaned up more barf, and many a night carried his little baby boy up and down the hallway rhythmically singing, "Yaaah-yah . . . yaaaah-yah . . . yaaah-yah . . . " until Ben fell asleep—most of the time.

When Ben grew big enough to tackle the canyons and hills surrounding our home, the two of them would hike together and share the sights, sounds, smells, and conversation that make up the heavenly stuff of father-and-son memories. Above all, Ben remembers learning to play soccer, because it was his dad who first taught him how. The world refers to it as the "Beautiful Game," but for Ben, its beauty is really his boyhood connection to his dad.

Passion for the game followed him through the years. His hopes to play soccer in college were realized, but injuries and circumstances beyond his control prevented the culmination of dreams that had begun in our backyard so many years before. He wanted to play for his dad. He wanted to be *excellent* and honor him and persevered through four years of some unbearable conditions and crises to do so, but it was not to be. The captain of the soccer team grieved the loss of his last year of college soccer and, with it, his dad. His heart told him that letting go of soccer meant letting go of his dad, and he couldn't see how doing such a thing was possible.

One night we sat together with worn spirits and bowed for comfort and direction. God spoke to us that night, and the vision He gave is one for the ages. A borderless room appeared to me, and it shone with gold. A large crucible sat in the middle of the room filled with liquid treasure. The one attending the gold's purification process was familiar; it was Jesus. He smiled and ceremoniously skimmed the dross off the top of the gold with His own hand and told me the gold was Ben's grief, and He said, "He gets to keep it." What Jesus skimmed off the top was the part of Ben's grief that was serving no purpose anymore. The portion of grief that remained was Ben's to keep, but it was time to purify his treasure. The Lord assured us that He would take care of the task Himself; Ben wouldn't have to do it. He just needed to trust.

Refining metal with fire is one of the oldest methods known to man and is still in use today. Flames need to reach over 1,000 degrees Celsius for dross to rise to the top, but there is no loss in value to the remaining gold throughout the process, only increase in its worth and potential. Dross is considered a contaminant and must be removed, or the value of the precious metal will be lost.[44] To "refine" something literally means to free it and to improve it for the purpose of *excellence*. In Greek it translates "to be ignited." Fittingly, the symbol for gold (Au) comes from the Latin word meaning "shining or glowing dawn," because during the final stages of refining, the gold experiences what is called a "brightening." This phenomenon occurs when the last impurities vanish and the pure metal emits a bright flash of light.

The vision from that evening's time of sorrow and prayer continues to teach. We don't miss the dross at all. It is made up of useless waste and keeps a broken heart from healing. Leaving it behind has never seemed painful, nor does it induce more grief, because the Master's hand does the work of it and sees to its completion.

My Persevering Friend, the only comfort you may have right now is the tears on your face, and looking forward to the seeming endlessness of it all holds no hope for the future. Passions and dreams may have ended in your backyard too, and memories may haunt you instead of heal, but the compassionate flame of your Refiner will not leave you with riches that cannot be used. His love will not allow waste to tarnish your worth or potential. The treasure of your grief will remain to accomplish its purpose, but what is useless, what will not produce anything of value, what will contaminate your future must be entrusted to the refining hand of Jesus. You cannot separate the dross yourself; it is too difficult, but that's okay. Everything is difficult right now, so one less thing to handle is healing in itself and is your respite. The refining will continue throughout the life of your grief, but when it has been tried, you will come forth as gold.

Ben wanted to play soccer to honor his dad because he wanted to be *excellent* for him. In God's providence, to be refined and live without the dross of grief means to be free, to be improved, and to be *excellent*. It looks like Ben's dream did come true. No wonder Jesus was smiling.

But He knows the way that I take. [He has concern for it, appreciates, and pays attention to it.] When He has tried me, I shall come forth as refined gold [pure and luminous].
Job 23:10 AMP

I have held many things in my hands and I have lost them all. But whatever I have placed in God's hands, that I still possess.
Martin Luther

Thirty-Nine

Blossoms

For behold, the winter is past; the rain is over and gone; the flowers have already appeared in the land; the time has arrived for pruning the vines, and the voice of the turtledove has been heard in our land. The fig tree has ripened its figs, and the vines in blossom have given forth their fragrance. Arise, my darling, my beautiful one, and come along.

Song of Solomon 2:11–13 NASB

the almond trees at the bottom of the mountain were always the first to blossom. Every spring I looked forward to their display because it meant winter was losing its hold. The highway down into the Kern Valley curved and meandered a bit in an effort to conceal the coming landscape, but around the last bend and shoulder awaited the promised blossoms as far as one could see.

That April was different. We drove down the familiar road into the warm valley to take care of funeral arrangements. Despite Bob's death and against my wishes, the almond trees blossomed early as usual, held out their white-petaled welcome, and escorted our sorrow with the sun.

The almond tree is known as the "wakeful tree" because it awakens from winter's sleep earlier than others. In Hebrew, *almond* means "the awakening one," and with the tree's inaugural declaration each spring, it testifies of the power of the light to which it opens its beauty. In the same way, the tabernacle's lamp stand extended its seven golden branches up into cups made in the forms of open almond flowers commissioned to hold the small bowls of oil and wicks that were lit and never to go out.[45] And in the book of Numbers, Aaron's rod is described as an almond branch that, though it was cut off and dead, miraculously burgeoned with buds, blossoms, and ripe almonds.

I don't live there on the mountain anymore and seldom have the chance to drive down into the valley, but I do sit now to write at a lovely table hand-painted by my best friend Carla. It is embellished with different shades of white and blushing-pink flowers that look like almond blossoms and frame the words "In Thee do I put my trust." A willow leans over a small creek in our yard, and it is spring. Though its boughs weep, they are green with new life and are harbingers of the shade we will enjoy soon under the summer heat.

My Friend, what is around the bend and shoulder of your promenade may not be in sight yet, but the display must endure its seasons before fruit can be seen. The aching limbs of your grief may even feel broken off and dead, but you will lift your head and raise your arms soon enough, and you will carry the light that is never to go out. You will weep, but your tears will sow new life. Winter will pass, and the rains will be over and gone. The flowers will appear in the land, and the time will come to prune the vines and sing. There will be fragrance again, my Dear Believing Friend, and your Beloved will say to you, "Arise, My darling, My beautiful one, and come along."

Forty

Endurance

It's like in the great stories, Mr. Frodo. The ones that really mattered. Full of darkness and danger they were. And sometimes you didn't want to know the end . . . because how could the end be happy? How could the world go back to the way it was when so much bad had happened? But in the end, it's only a passing this . . . this shadow. Even darkness must pass. A new day will come. And when the sun shines, it will shine out the clearer. Those were the stories that stayed with you. That meant something, even if you were too small to understand why. But I think, Mr. Frodo, I do understand. I know now. Folk in those stories

*had lots of chances of turning back, only they didn't. They
kept going, because they were holding on to something.*
J. R. R. Tolkien, *The Lord of the Rings: The Two Towers*

biblically, the number forty represents rain and floods, wanderings and wilderness, Mount Sinai, Nineveh, the reign of Saul, David and Solomon, manna, and Jesus' days of fasting and temptation in the desert. Goliath taunted Israel for forty days until he met his demise in a shepherd boy (whose great-grandmother was a widow, by the way), and Jesus stayed on earth for forty days after His resurrection to assure His followers and skeptics of His great victory over sin and death. He also stayed to teach and prepare them for what was to come. Maybe, as Samwise said in *The Two Towers*, He stayed to make sure we all had something to hold on to, and then, when He went to build our final home, He left His Spirit, His breath, to get us through and so that our story would be one that would stay—one that would mean something.

Hebrew scholars say that forty is the thirteenth Hebraic letter *mem*, the letter of "water." It represents the idea of an underground spring that rises up and is the number for transition, change, renewal, or a new beginning.[46] Forty seems to symbolize times of necessity: sometimes of hardship and purging, sometimes of restoration and revival or the fulfillment of a promise. Its times can be full of explanation or mystery. There are two forms of *mem*, depending on how it is written. One is "open" and stands for the revealed truth of God, and one is "closed," standing for the concealed truth of God. So much of this life remains a mystery, but there is so much that is ours to know. All of it is God's and held in His care, including the revealed and concealed of your future.

And so, Dear Friend, we come back to where we began: the power of a story, the moments that define a life, and breathing. You have already endured so much more than I will ever know, and here you are at *your forty*. Whether this is the first task you have undergone and completed since your husband's death or you are further down the path in your grief, this is now *your forty*. I knew you could do it. Don't underestimate its significance. You have undergone, lasted, lived through, survived, persisted, and persevered, and because you have, your story will continue. It will breathe life into others because it is the *ruach*, the breath of God, who has brought you here. You have endured, and so will your testimony.

You have become more fluent in your new language of "widow"; you have transitioned and walked through the unknowns of grief. You have worshipped and settled a bit, forgiven, cast off blame and regret, and wept alone and in the dark. You have found treasure where you did not expect and have begun the reconstruction process with the tools of grace and gratitude. You have said more good-byes, and part of your new role has been defined and confirmed. You've received a standing ovation and maybe even danced a little. Well done. I mean that. I know a small part of what it has cost you, and I know you've had to endure a lot of pain to do it.

My Friend, you have held your breath and held onto your Christ, and soon the purpose for which He has set you apart will be revealed. He has and will continue to breathe into the dry bones of your grief, and you will live and be part of the great number of God's greatest allies. Your story will embrace others and show them what it means to pray and not lose heart because you have chosen Jesus, and you haven't turned back even though you wanted to. Your defining moments will help others define theirs, and the comfort you have received will comfort and multiply outward and into heaven.

The pages have turned and your life after his last breath has begun. Going on from here will be your bravest moment. Remember, there are other widows who need to breathe, and they need your air, your story, so that they can breathe too.

Keep breathing and find out how you
can help other widows breathe too:
www.mattersoflifeandbreath.com

About the Author

Susan VandePol created the Families of the Fallen protocol for fire departments and its congruent protocol, Life After Breath, for churches after the duty-related death of her husband to ALS in 2005. The protocol is now being used across the country and is endorsed by experts in the fields of grief, crisis, trauma, suicide prevention, CIR, PTSD, and CISM. Susan is certified in grief, crisis, and trauma counseling; grief coaching; master life coaching; individual crisis intervention; victim response; and basic and family mediation. Her speaking engagements have included numerous women's retreats and conferences, a keynote at the ICISF World Congress, and addressing the honor guard at the International Association of Firefighters Memorial. She homeschooled her three children without ever succumbing to pressure to wear Birkenstocks and now lives with her husband, whom she shamelessly manipulated into falling in love with her. He obliged by sweeping her off her feet with a large broom. They now reside in Michigan.

To contact Susan, view the Life After Breath protocol for your church, or for information on booking her to speak at your event, visit her website at www.mattersoflifeandbreath. com or www.familiesofthefallen.net.

Email Susan at lifeafterbreath@hotmail.com.

Follow Susan on Facebook and LinkedIn.

Acknowledgments

To the ones who helped us catch our breath:

Carla Muller

Merry Hagenston Bettie Clark

Roland, Carla, Nathanael, Jade, Adam and Sebastian Muller, Desiré Cooper, Rich and Leah Smith, Bob Heartsill, Andrew and Susan Daymude and family, Tony and Ellen Perone and family, Tom Lahey, Steve and Kris Weprin and family, and our dear Ortega family.

The Los Angeles City Fire Department, Los Angeles Firemen's Relief Association, and Local 112. Deron Jones, Tommy Reyes, Dave Perez, Ben Kuzichev, Pat Stilson, Pat Mckosker, Steve Tufts, Jim Vlach, Chief Bill and Liz Bamatre,

Ken Buzzell, Donnie McCullough, Fire Station 93 and the Dinosaurs.

The Kern County Fire Department

The Ventura County Fire Department

Calvary Chapel Frazier Park, Crossroads Christian Fellowship, Westbrook Chapel

Chris and Cappie Craft and family, all the Berkowitz/Wada family, Chuck and Linda McDaniel and family, Mike Kelly and family, Logan Kelly, Clay Worrell and family, Joe Moore, Steve Ogden, L. J. Lara, Ron and Barbara Edsall, John and Jessica DeYoung and family, Tim and Donna Ellis and family, Scott Jones and family, Chris and Sandy Snow, Sally Betters, Scott Cunningham, Tommy Heil, Alicia Jewett, Dave and Nancy Cariker, Don, Bettie, Josh and Meemz Clark, Paul Shedd, Paul Gizzi, the Southern California Seahorses, Adam Frye, Hoffman Hospice, Melinda Moustakis, Carrie Squires, Holly Harrison.

To my children Jennifer Marie, Samuel Robert, and Benjamin Victor: During the time you saw your dad at his worst and watched him fade into eternity, he saw you at your best and watched you press through and live. It didn't feel like it at the time, I know. You felt helpless and sometimes numb or frozen with emotion. He worried about you, of course, but with the confidence of a dad who knew the faithfulness of his God. Amidst his humiliation, he despised the pain you had to endure because of him, but he admired you more than you will ever know because of it too. Your steadfast love and loyalty to him, to me, to each other, and to your God was your greatest gift to the man whose legacy you carry, and you do it better than anyone I've ever known. Bob Ortega lives on in your faces, mannerisms, talents, voices, gifts, and most importantly your faith. You honored him, comforted him, watched him fall, listened to the sounds of his illness in the night, released him, and sang him to heaven. He persevered under trial, was approved, and received his crown of life that the Lord had promised him. Now, though he be dead, yet still he speaks . . . in you. I love you more than life and breath.

To my son-in-law Lee Briggs and daughter-in-law Cheyene Ortega: You are the answered prayer of your spouses' dad and mom, and God couldn't have chosen anyone better. You are the best, and I'm honored to call you my family. Bob's life lives on in you now, and I know he'd be honored too.

To the future Mrs. Ben, whoever you are . . . we can't wait to love you.

We love you, Zoe Abigail and Havalah Jane. We wish you could have known your grandpa, but you will. That will be a great day.

To Bob VandePol, my husband and very own Dutchman: You have been "the rest of me" from the first moment I saw you, and you have been my "welcome home" ever since. I could never have imagined "masculine" being lived out in such beauty, but there you were. You are my fairy tale and battleground. You have more than loved me and have turned my wasteland of grief into tall grasses and a lake breeze. Grief and gratitude brought us together, and now you are my pillar, come what may. This book would never have happened were it not for you. May I live in a manner worthy of the gift you are.

Thank you to all the wonderful VandePol family. You have embraced this California girl unconditionally and with grace. I am indebted and love you deeply.

To the staff at Morgan James: Terry Whalin, your kindness and thoughtfulness had me from the start. Thank you. David Hancock, Jim Howard, Tiffany Gibson, Bethany Marshall: I just love you all, and am humbled to know you and to be a part of the family there at Morgan James. Thank you for being honorable, honest, and accessible with a balance of professionalism and humor thrown in. Thank you for your warmth to this newcomer and for taking such good care of me and of my message.

To Amanda Rooker at SplitSeed: You are so much more than an editor. I can't imagine having another editor for this project. Thank you for pouring yourself into the spoken and unspoken words of this book. You have become a part of its message, an answered prayer, and a part of my life. Thank you to Angie Kiesling of SplitSeed for following the call to finish it all up. I knew your heart was in it from the start, and I know you felt it was yours to do.

To the ones who have breathed their last:

Samuel M. Weprin, Jean Weprin, Baby Ortega, Juan Ortega, Casi Ortega, Robby Duncan, Joe Cooper, Tom Lahey, Angela Russo, Reuben Weprin, Jack Tropp, Lillian Tropp, Danielle Marie Gould, Benjamin Gavriel Blackwood, Jake Cariker, Peggy Turner, Anthony King, Eddie Joe Bowers, Art and Margriet van de Pol, Nanning and Johanna Vegter, Jesse Patrick Buist, Ryan Michael Davis, Aurora Skye Nickerson,

Elijah Praise Nickerson, Alex Borgia, Jenny Henderson, and *Rudy*.

Endnotes

1   Source: hebrew4christians.com.

2   Source: *New American Standard New Testament Greek Lexicon.*

3   Albert Barnes, *Barnes's Notes on the New Testament: 1 Corinthians to Galatians* (Baker, 2005 reprint), 40-41.

4   "What It Is to Remember (and to Forget)" in "Sermons and Writings of Victor Shepherd," victorshepherd.ca.

5   1 Thessalonians 4:13 NIV.

6   1 Thessalonians 4:14–18 NLT.

7   John 14:1–3 NLT.

8   1 Corinthians 15:51 NLT.

9   Matthew 24:31 NLT.

10   1 Corinthians 15:54–57 NLT.

11 Philippians 3:20 NASB.

12 Source: Joann Bodurtha, MD, professor of human genetics at Virginia Commonwealth University.

13 Francois Champoux and Simon Landry, University of Montreal, *NBC News*, May 18, 2012.

14 Kristoffer Nyrop, *The Kiss and Its History* (Nabu Press, 2010).

15 John Piper, www.desiringGod.com.

16 Ibid.

17 Hauser et al, "Ligament Injury and Healing: A Review of Current Clinical Diagnostics and Therapeutics," *The Open Rehabilitation Journal*, 2013.

18 Sources: Timothy Hewitt, PhD, and Christopher Kaeding, MD, Ohio State University, 2013.

19 David Weinstock, "The Heart—An Organ of Perception," Liminal Somatics, December 28, 2011, http://liminalsomatics.com/the-heart-an-organ-of-perception.

20 Emilio Ferrer, David Sbarra, and J. L. Helm, "Assessing Cross-Partner Associations in Physiological Responses via Coupled Oscillator Models," *American Psychological Association Journal*, September 12, 2011.

21 Source: John J. Parsons, hebrew4christians.com.

22 Although I could not find it published in any written source, this quotation has been attributed to J. B. Lightfoot.

23 Source: biblehub.com.

24 Kumi O. Kuroda et al, "Infant Calming Responses during Maternal Carrying in Humans and Mice," *Current Biology*, April 19, 2013.

25   Sophie Schwartz, Laurence Bayer, Irena Constantinescu, Stephen Perrig, Julie Vienne, Pierre-Paul Vidal, and Michael Muhlethaler, "Rocking Synchronizes Brain Waves during a Short Nap," *Current Biology,* June 21, 2011.

26   Ibid.

27   Y. S. Heo, L. M. Cabrera, C. L. Bormann, C. T. Shah, S. Takayama, and G. D. Smith, "Dynamic Microfunnel Culture Enhances Embryo Development and Pregnancy Rates," *Human Reproduction* 25, No. 3, pp. 613–622.

28   From the hymn "Be Still, My Soul," words by Katharina A. von Schlegel.

29   *Easton's Bible Dictionary,* Third Edition (1897), Theopedia.com.

30   *Barnes's Notes on the Old Testament.*

31   Adam Clarke, Matthew 11:28-30 Commentary, preceptaustin.com, May 17, 2014.

32   Rick Renner, *Sparkling Gems from the Greek* (Teach All Nations Publishing, 2003).

33   L. O. Richards, *Expository Dictionary of Bible Words* (Regency, 1985).

34   Source: etymonline.com.

35   Source: freedictionary.com.

36   Source: preceptaustin.org.

37   Source: dictionary.com.

38   Ibid.

39   Ibid.

40   Ibid.

41   Ibid.

42 *John Gill's Exposition on the Entire Bible,* Kindle edition (Graceworks Multimedia, 2011).

43 C. H. Spurgeon, "The Shameful Sufferer: A Sermon" (No. 236), delivered at the Music Hall, Royal Surrey Gardens, January 30, 1859, The Spurgeon Archive, http://www. spurgeon.org/sermons/0236.htm.

44 Source: wiki.answers.com.

45 Source: bible-history.com.

46 Source: www.hebrew4christians.com.

And I, brethren, when I came to you, did not come with excellence of speech or of wisdom declaring to you the testimony of God. For I determined not to know anything among you except Jesus Christ and Him crucified. I was with you in weakness, in fear, and in much trembling. And my speech and my preaching were not with persuasive words of human wisdom, but in demonstration of the Spirit and of power, that your faith should not be in the wisdom of men but in the power of God.

1 Corinthians 2:1–5 NKJV

CPSIA information can be obtained at www.ICGtesting.com
Printed in the USA
BVOW02s2116020415

394479BV00002B/2/P

9 781630 473426